CULTURE ON THE MOVING FRONTIER

LOUIS B. WRIGHT

Culture on the
Moving Frontier

HARPER TORCHBOOKS / The Academy Library

HARPER & BROTHERS, NEW YORK

CULTURE ON THE MOVING FRONTIER

Copyright © 1955 by Indiana University Press
Printed in the United States of America

This book was originally published in 1955 by Indiana University Press and is here reprinted by arrangement.

This book is also available in a hardcover edition published by Indiana University Press.

First HARPER TORCHBOOK *edition published 1961.*

Library of Congress catalog card number: 54-6207

THE PATTEN FOUNDATION

Mr. Will Patten of Indianapolis (A.B., Indiana University, 1893) made, in 1931, a gift for the establishment of the Patten Foundation at his Alma Mater. Under the terms of this gift, which became available upon the death of Mr. Patten (May 3, 1936), there is to be chosen each year a Visiting Professor who is to be in residence several weeks during the year. The purpose of this prescription is to provide an opportunity for members and friends of the University to enjoy the privilege and advantage of personal acquaintance with the Visiting Professor. The Visiting Professor for the Patten Foundation in 1952-53 was

DR. LOUIS B. WRIGHT

Preface

SO MUCH has been written in recent years about the disparate quality of American society, about its conflicting elements and its unassimilated groups, that we sometimes forget that we are really a remarkably homogeneous people. That homogeneity is all the more remarkable when we consider the diverse national and racial groups who compose the population of the United States. No country has ever before taken so many different peoples, speaking so many different languages, and in so short a time assimilated them into one nation with a common tongue and a common denominator of social attitudes and outlook. Despite political differences over which we argue at times with considerable violence, despite an enormous variety of religions, and despite many economic and social variations, we have become a people fundamentally unified. Only during the past few years, under the lash of political demagoguery, have we been so frightened and divided that our unity is threatened.

The pattern of American society which accounts for our social unification was established in the colonial period and continued during the nineteenth century as we expanded westward. The purpose of the following chapters is to indicate the nature of the struggle to reproduce the best of an older culture which the settlers in a new country remembered and treasured.

The six chapters presented here are lectures delivered

on the Patten Foundation at Indiana University in the spring of 1953. They are printed as delivered. To have attempted to expand the lecture form would have been to write another kind of book. Obviously in six lectures, one cannot deal with all the frontier zones or with all the subtle variations in the social development of many differing regions. What I have tried to do is to choose what seemed to me the most important elements in the regions which had the greatest influence in the development of the country. The most significant cultural element in determining our homogeneity was what, for want of a better term, we may loosely describe as the Anglo-Saxon tradition, the tradition of English law, the English language, English literature, and British religion and customs. I have tried to suggest the importance of these factors. To discuss these matters in detail would require many volumes and would duplicate material already in print.

I wish to express my profound appreciation to President Herman B Wells of Indiana University, to the Patten Committee, and particularly to its chairman, Professor Stith Thompson, and to all those members of the faculty at Indiana University who listened and gave advice. I am also grateful to my friend, Henry Allen Moe, for wise criticism and counsel. To my assistant, Virginia Freund, I am under a special obligation. Her learning and sound sense were of immense help in the preparation of these lectures.

LOUIS B. WRIGHT

The Folger Library, Washington, D. C.

Contents

CULTURE ON THE MOVING FRONTIER

ONE

The Colonial Struggle Against Barbarism

THE struggle between the good and evil angels for the soul of man was a popular theme in medieval drama. English audiences about 1425 delighted in a play called *The Castle of Perseverance* in which the Seven Virtues and the Four Daughters of God defended the fortress against the Devil and the Seven Deadly Sins who were determined to capture Mankind and make him their own. Although we have long since forgotten the old play, we are still witnesses of the perennial struggle for man's soul. Indeed, the development of American society from the first settlement at Jamestown until the latest outpost in the Far West has exemplified the contest between the powers of darkness and the forces of light for the soul and mind of the American citizen. The history of society on the ever moving frontier might well be cast in the metaphor of this morality play. As we have grown increasingly more secular, the dramatis personae have concerned themselves with the minds rather than the souls of men, but the two can never be separated. Under whatever names the contestants may be called, the conflict goes on.

The freedom, the lack of restraint, and the lawlessness of the American frontier have received such dramatic emphasis in the literature describing the movement of settlers across this continent that we are prone to forget other more significant characteristics. We are likely to overlook the unspectacular efforts of godly and law-abiding folk to establish old patterns of behavior. Yet on every frontier, as the American continent was settled, a group who sometimes described themselves self-consciously as the "better element" waged a persistent warfare against the disintegrating forces which the liberty of a wild country unloosed. This group were the conservators of traditional conduct, traditional ways of doing things, traditional manners and morals, and they sought to preserve and perpetuate the ancient inheritance of things of the mind and spirit. In short, they tried to reproduce in the new environment the best of the civilized way of life they had previously known. Sometimes this better element was a minority, but a potent minority who, if they lost an occasional battle, usually managed in some fashion to win the war against the powers of darkness. The conservation and perpetuation of traditional civilization in each newly settled region of the country have not received dramatic acclaim; they are not the subjects for stirring novels or sensational movies; but few characteristics have had a greater importance in the development of American society as we know it today.

The ideas and traditions that determined the quality of American character were, of course, British, for the dominant stock in the colonial period was British. Other nations and races contributed their quotas to the early settlements, but at most their influence merely modified prevailing British characteristics. Although French Huguenots, German Pietists, Dutch Calvinists, and other non-British groups played a prominent part in the development of certain regions, their cultures flourished only in relatively small areas and in time were enveloped or overlaid with elements of British civilization.

British culture has demonstrated a remarkable vitality, and an even more remarkable capacity for the assimilation and transformation of other cultures into the British pattern. For example, despite the large proportion of Dutch in New York, that colony, by the end of the seventeenth century, had already absorbed so much from its English conquerors that it could not be thought of as an alien land. It had become an English colony, and Dutchmen in New York City had begun to ape English fashions. If certain characteristics of Dutch architecture, of Dutch cooking, and of Dutch folklore became a part of the permanent inheritance of New York, nevertheless the prevailing influences were British. The Dutch inheritance served merely to give a special flavor to British culture which took root and flourished in New York. So it was in all of the thirteen colonies, and in the later colonies which they in turn sent out to people the rest of the American continent. Many races and nationalities contributed to the stream of settlers who went West, and many influences modified the mode of life which they adopted, but the vigor of British culture was such that it gave to all the cities and towns along the route of the westward migration a characteristic stamp. Different as are Philadelphia, New York, Boston, Cincinnati, Lexington, Indianapolis, St. Louis, San Francisco, and Seattle, they all have a cultural common denominator that goes back to the seventeenth century and the stock of ideas that British settlers brought with them.

These ideas were a part of an ancient inheritance which had been greatly enriched in the sixteenth century when Englishmen responded to a new spirit alive in the world. They had wakened to a fresh realization of the interest and importance of the world across the Channel. They had also become aware of the value of Spanish gold from the New World, and they took what they considered a proper share of this wealth. But English acquisitiveness was not confined to the material riches of gold and silver. They pillaged the intellectual closets of Europe and brought home ideas and information which stimulated all England and brought about a Golden Age of literature and learning. Stirred to the depths of its soul by the religious revolution taking place in Europe, England underwent a transformation in its spiritual life. The controversies and ideological conflicts that the Reformation unleashed affected every phase of English life for two centuries, and in time influenced the quality of American civilization. For these and many other reasons, students of American history should begin their studies, not with the settlement of Jamestown, or even with Raleigh's abortive attempts at colonization, but with the intellectual and spiritual upheavals in Europe that began in the late fifteenth century and gathered force during the next century and a half. Most of the ideas that our colonial ancestors brought with them received their modern shape in this period.

Modern America is so polyglot, and social historians have devoted so much attention in recent years to analyzing and describing the multifarious European, Asiatic, and African influences in the development of American life that we are now in danger of under-estimating and even of forgetting the oldest, the most persistent, and the most vigorous strain in our cultural inheritance.[1] Great Britain's influence is still so strong that it subtly determines qualities of mind and character in Americans who cannot claim a drop of Anglo-Saxon blood. This is not to say that these influences necessarily make Americans pro-English. Colonel Mc-Cormick and his Anglophobe confreres in the *Chicago Tribune*'s empire need have no worries about the un-American nature of this foreign element. Indeed, they are just as much under its spell as any others, even if they do not know it or would not admit it. If there were no other legacy from the past except the English language and its literature, that alone would be sufficient to explain the durability and strength of the tradition.

The long struggle to transplant a civilized way of life to the wilderness began with the arrival of the

first Englishmen at Jamestown in 1607, and the nature
of that struggle was characteristic of that which went
on in many later wilderness communities. The early
settlers were an unruly lot, more intent upon finding
gold or some other quick source of wealth, than upon
establishing a stable society. Yet they were not so far
gone in greed and sin that they forgot to bring along
a parson, one Robert Hunt; and perhaps the first permanent structure erected at Jamestown was a church.

These men, living in a pestilential marsh within
earshot and bowshot of the Indians, were not allowed
to lapse into savagery. When Captain John Smith sent
a detail of gentlemen to chop wood, they blistered
their hands and swore at the pain, an offense against
decorum which caused their commander to decree a
proper punishment—a can of cold water poured down
the offender's sleeve for each oath. The picture of
Captain Smith or his deputy counting oaths and meting
out punishment has in it the elements of comic opera,
but it signifies a determination to whip the lawless
pioneers into an ordered and decent community.

The rough settlement at Jamestown was not altogether destitute of the symbols of a cultivated life, for
the parson, Master Hunt, brought along a library,
which, unhappily, he lost by fire, and the next preacher,
the Reverend Richard Buck, also had a "library of
books." John Pory, a bibulous secretary who came over
with Sir George Yeardley in 1619, wrote back to Sir
Dudley Carleton that books would be his solace against
loneliness in Jamestown, for he had resolved "to mind

my own business here, and next after my pen, to have some good book always in store, being in solitude the best and choicest company." [2] He was more fortunate than another settler, one Jacob Bradshaw, who a little later sought the comfort of literature but "received his death at the hands of God by lightning and thunder of heaven as he was lying on a chest and reading in a book." Even literary composition was not unknown in the early days of Jamestown, for not only did some of the newcomers sit down and write back descriptions of the new country, but George Sandys even took time out in 1622 to work on his translation of Ovid's *Metamorphoses,* the earliest contribution to belles-lettres in the English-speaking colonies.

Amidst bitter quarrels, mismanagement, hunger, and death from disease and Indian attacks, the earliest frontiersmen did not completely lose touch with civilization. The majority of the original colonists, to be sure, had small concern with anything except their immediate physical welfare, but a few kept alive the memory of the essentials of a cultivated life. Within a decade after the first settler stepped ashore at Jamestown, a movement was under way to found schools in the colony. By royal decree the Bishops at home collected money for Virginia schools and on May 26, 1619, Sir Edwin Sandys, the treasurer of the Virginia Company, could boast the sum of £1,500 for "that pious work." The Company set aside ten thousand acres for "the university to be planted at Henrico" and another thousand acres for a "college for the conversion of the infidels." Not only were Englishmen in Virginia to be educated but the Indians as well were to share in the benefits of learning, which the seventeenth century equated with godliness.

These ventures attracted so much attention in the next few years that Virginia's education became a favored charity. The Reverend Patrick Copland, chaplain of the East Indiaman, the "Royal James," took up a collection while that vessel was lying off the Cape of Good Hope in 1621 and was able to transmit to the Virginia Company £70 8s. 6d. which could be used to build a church or a school. It is worthy of note that the officers of the Company decided that a school would be more beneficial and ordered a "public free school, which, being for the education of children and grounding them in the principles of religion, civility of life, and humane learning, served to carry with it the greatest weight and highest consequence unto the plantations." [3]

Although the chief propaganda for Virginia schools, it is true, came from people in England, a few of the colonists themselves helped to further the cause. One of the most famous free schools in Virginia was founded as early as 1635 by the will of Benjamin Symmes, a planter who had done so well that he left two hundred acres of land and eight cows to support a school for children from Elizabeth City and Kiquotan parishes. The education of the Indians, however, for all of the talk about this enterprise, made no headway. The colonists' hope of solving the Indian problem through the pious instruction of the infidels' children vanished in the massacre of 1622 when the Indians fell on the outlying settlements and nearly wiped out the infant colony. The devastation of the college lands gave the projected university at Henrico such a blow that it never recovered.

The plantation system which developed in Virginia and Maryland was not the sort of society calculated to produce a sophisticated culture, and it is proof of the hardiness of the cultural organism that this region actually did see the transplanting of so much of the learning and literate interests which characterized seventeenth- and eighteenth-century England. Instead of settling in towns, the colonists in the Chesapeake Bay area fanned out along the rivers and creeks and established themselves on tobacco farms, invariably called plantations in this region.

In a country cut by rivers and creeks, the waterways became the principal means of transportation, and ships from London and Bristol tied up at the planter's own dock. He shipped his tobacco direct to England and ordered everything he needed from his agent overseas, even leaving to his factor's discretion the choice of a new dress for his wife or a hair ribbon for his daughter. Such conditions of trade discouraged the growth of towns, and towns are generally considered necessary for the development of learning, literature, music, and the arts.

These flowers of civilization do not flourish in the cold isolation of the country but require the hothouse air of cities. Even pastoral poetry, which glorifies country life and romanticizes dairymaids, shepherds, and shepherdesses, is written by city dwellers nostalgic for a rural existence that never was. If a dirt farmer has anything to do with dairymaids, shepherds, or shepherdesses, his interests are not likely to run to sentimental reveries or poetry in any meter.

Frontier farmers—and that is what the Virginia and Maryland planters were—of necessity led a busy life. Even when the tobacco planters had laborers, white or slave, to do the roughest work, they nevertheless had an unending task of supervision. If a planter expected to prosper, he had to give his personal attention to the planting and cultivation of the crops, the erection of houses and barns, the preparation and shipping of the tobacco, keeping accounts and records, even the care of the servants themselves, not to mention the bringing up of his children, and public and civic responsibilities. There was no time on a plantation for conventional pastoralism, and precious little time for the cultivation of the mind.

Faced with the hard life exacted by an agricultural economy, weak or indolent folk might have lapsed into barbarism. But the men and women who established themselves in this country were neither weak nor lazy, and they had an almost grim determination to reproduce modes of life which they had respected and honored in the old country. Civilization did not come to the river lands of Virginia and Maryland as a spontaneous growth. It was cultivated with even greater effort than the planters gave to the growing of tobacco and livestock. Men and women worked hard to retain their own intellectual and spiritual inheritance and to pass on to their children the accomplishments and qualities of character which they most admired.

The development of the Tidewater aristocracy in the Chesapeake Bay area is proof of the vitality of the concepts of the country families in England, the country gentry. Pretentious as are the genealogies of many Virginia families, actually their origins are extremely vague. Though many of them think they are descended from some noble or royal ancestor—King Edward III is frequently claimed—most of them have no clear proof of their ancestry on the other side of the Atlantic. Their first American ancestors were immigrants hoping to improve their economic lot, like immigrants in any age; they would not have left England had they been important or prosperous. Marcus Jernegan, weary with listening to fabulous genealogies, once remarked that if Virginians would quit looking for their ancestors in Burke's peerage and start searching the calendars of Newgate Prison they would come nearer finding them.[4] But who the Virginians were before they came to this country is less important than what they became once they were here. Those with enough capital or influence to acquire substantial holdings of land quickly set about establishing themselves as country gentlemen as nearly like the county families of England as they could make themselves. The son of a London grocer or ship chandler, once he had lands in the New World, translated himself into a gentleman, and soon was trying to acquire the accomplishments befitting his station.

The Byrd family is an excellent illustration of this upward progress. They did not reach their social eminence without exertion but their evolution is characteristic of the growth of the new agrarian aristocracy. The first William Byrd was the son of a London goldsmith who married the daughter of a ship captain in the Virginia trade. Sometime around 1670 young Byrd went to Virginia to live with an uncle who had acquired land which he bequeathed to his nephew. Byrd established a trading post on an inherited plantation in Henrico County, not far from the present site of Richmond, and became a shrewd Indian trader. His agents traversed the back country and exchanged pots, pans, guns, and rum for furs. He ran a store from which he supplied other planters with rum, molasses, sugar, barrel staves, household goods, and other products which he imported from the West Indies or England. He also became a slave trader. His land holdings were extensive, and he lavished especial attention on the estate at Westover on the James. But for all of his acquisitiveness and devotion to trade, he was not merely concerned with material things.

The elder William Byrd laid the foundation of the fine library which his son of the same name augmented until it was one of the best in the American colonies. He interested himself in education and served on the building committee of the College of William and Mary, founded in 1693. Lest his own children should grow up uncouth and untrained, he sent William, Susan, and Ursula, the eldest of whom was only a small child, to school in England. To his father-in-law in England, Byrd wrote in 1685 when Ursula was four years old: "My wife hath all this year urged me to send little Nutty [Ursula] home to you, to which I have at last condescended, and hope you'll please to excuse the trouble. I must confess she could learn nothing good here in a great family of Negroes." [5] The Byrds realized that a plantation on the outskirts of civilization, inhabited chiefly with slaves just imported from Africa, would not provide the best opportunities for their children and they were willing to risk separation and the hazards of travel across the Atlantic in order that their sons and daughters might receive a proper education.

The challenge of the wilderness was pressing and the response of planters like William Byrd—to use Mr. Toynbee's formula—demonstrated their zeal to overcome the hazards of their intractable environment. They were not going to allow their children to grow up barbarous in the backwoods of Virginia, not even if they had to jeopardize their lives by sending them overseas.

The second William Byrd of Westover in his devotion to learning showed the nature of his own response to the challenge. Young Byrd learned business practices from his father's agents in London, the firm of Perry & Lane. He also became a member of the Middle Temple where he made friends with literary figures like Congreve, Wycherley, and Nicholas Rowe. A persistent social climber, Byrd also scraped acquaintance with a long roster of nobles and gentry, some of whose portraits he had painted and brought home to West-over where they long served to impress home-keeping Virginians. Byrd's scientific interests were sufficient to gain admittance to the Royal Society where he read a paper on an albino Negro whom he had closely observed.

During a long career devoted to public service in Virginia, William Byrd never relaxed in his effort to maintain his own scholarship and learning. His splendid library at Westover was useful to his neighbors, though Byrd often grudged the loan of a book to a careless friend who might not return it. Thanks to a diary in which he made daily entries we know something of the pleasure which that library gave him, and we also realize the discipline which Byrd imposed upon himself to retain his skill in languages and his familiarity with classical literature. A typical entry, for June 17, 1710, reads:

"I rose about 5 o'clock and read two chapters in Hebrew and 200 verses in Homer. I said my prayers and ate milk for breakfast. . . . I wrote a letter about my father Parke's will and desired Mr. Perry to give me [credit] for the £1000 which my father Parke ordered him to pay me. I ate roast mutton for dinner. . . . Then I wrote a letter to Mrs. Custis and another to Captain Posford to desire him to deliver my letters at Williamsburg, and his seaman came for them.

I read some French till the evening, and then took a walk about the plantation with my wife. Then we returned and ate some milk. Just as we went to bed it began to rain exceedingly and thundered. I said a short prayer and had good health, good thoughts, and good humor, thank God Almighty." [6]

Almost daily, year in and year out, Byrd forced himself to read a little Greek, Latin, and Hebrew. Occasionally he read French or Italian to keep up with the modern tongues. Although a James River plantation in the early eighteenth century was no longer on the literal frontier, it was still remote from the sophistication of cities. It required an effort, beyond that which most men would exert, for Byrd to remain a student of languages and literature and at the same time carry on the busy life of a planter and man of affairs. Finding himself marooned at "Tuckahoe," the Randolph plantation, then in the back country, where he was visiting certain mines, Byrd entertained himself and his hosts by reading aloud *The Beggar's Opera* and discussing comedy. When he was leader of a commission to survey the dividing line between Virginia and North Carolina in 1728, he kept a journal which he transformed into one of the most urbane pieces of writing in colonial America. Byrd brought to rural Virginia a little of the cultivation and literary taste of Augustan England.

The challenge of the wilderness which the Byrd family met so successfully presented a never-ending problem for planters bent upon establishing their families on fresh land in the Chesapeake Bay country.

Unless the planter was willing to sink to a level of sodden materialism, he had to keep up a continual struggle against the deadening influences of isolation, loneliness, and the lack of the kind of stimulation which might have come from intellectual associations. Sometimes the plantation environment was almost overwhelming. For example, William Fitzhugh, son of a woolen draper of Bedford, England, who established himself in the wilds of Stafford County, Virginia, in the 1670's, managed to accumulate a fortune, build himself a comfortable house, and surround himself with the trappings of gentility, but he was continually oppressed by the threat of a barbarizing environment. Perhaps the very consciousness of the hazard made him all the more diligent to guard against it. "Society that is good and ingenious," he wrote to a correspondent in London in 1687, "is very scarce and seldom to be come at except in books. Good education of children is almost impossible, and better be never born than ill-bred. But that which bears the greatest weight with me, for I look upon myself to be in my declining age, is the want of spiritual helps and comforts, of which this fertile country in everything else is barren and unfruitful." [7]

To guard against the ill-breeding of his son and heir, Fitzhugh was preparing to send the child, then just four years old, to England when he found a Huguenot minister who undertook to tutor the little boy in French and Latin. Finally when young William was eleven and a half, his father sent him to London with instructions for him to be given a thorough education in Latin, French, English, and other parts of good learning. The father's care was repaid, for the boy grew up to be one of the foremost gentlemen of Virginia and an ornament to the commonwealth.

The elder Fitzhugh imported good books and kept up a correspondence with his fellow Virginians which helped to alleviate the loneliness of his residence in Stafford County. His knowledge of the law was considerable, and his letters are full of commentary on legal theory. Isolated though he was, he helped to emphasize to his fellow planters the importance and the majesty of the English legal tradition as embodied in the common law. Statute law, he commented once to Richard Lee, cannot be understood properly unless one knows the body of the common law. This legal tradition, he insists, "is only to be learned out of ancient authors (for out of the old fields must come the new corn) contrary to opinion of the generality of our judges and practicers of the law here." [8]

Fitzhugh's friend Richard Lee, second of the name in this country, and the founder of the great Lee dynasty, was another who met the challenge of the wilderness and refused to succumb to a life barren of intellectual and spiritual satisfactions. Though Lee's plantation, "Mt. Pleasant," in Westmoreland County, on the Potomac River was then in a remote region, he brought together an excellent library which enabled him to combine the contemplative with the active life. Busy as he was as colonel of the militia, judge of the county court, collector of customs on the Potomac, and member of the Council of State, Lee nevertheless had time for scholarship. Indeed, the multiplicity of his accomplishments and the many sides of his personality make him an exemplification of the Renaissance type of gentleman. So great was his learning that he kept his ordinary notes in Latin, Greek, or Hebrew. When he died, his epitaph declared that "While he exercised the office of magistrate he was a zealous promoter of the public good. He was very skillful in the Greek and Latin languages and other parts of polite learning. He quietly resigned his soul to God, whom he always devoutly worshipped, on the 12th day of March, in the year 1714, in the 68th year of his age."

Lee's epitaph suggests the devotion to public service, learning, and religion which characterized the ideal behavior of the planters who were establishing the tradition of English culture in the Tidewater region. Not every planter, it is true, lived up to this high ideal, but the mere fact that it was an ideal and that many planters succeeded in some degree in putting such theories into practice resulted in the establishment of a remarkable society, a society which produced many notable leaders in the generations to come.

Those who failed to meet the challenge also produced a society of their own to which American folklore is much beholden. William Byrd encountered some of them in the backwoods of North Carolina when he was surveying the dividing line. Fertile soil and a benign climate made life so easy that these North

Carolinians succumbed to a slothful existence little better than that of the Indians. The men were accustomed to lie snoring in bed through the early hours of the day, Byrd writes. "Then, after Stretching and Yawning for half an Hour, they light their Pipes, and under the Protection of a cloud of Smoak, venture out into the open Air; tho', if it happens to be never so little cold, they quickly return Shivering into the Chimney corner. When the weather is mild, they stand leaning with both their arms upon the corn-field fence, and gravely consider whether they had best go and take a Small Heat at the Hough: but generally find reasons to put it off till another time. Thus they loiter away their Lives, like Solomon's Sluggard." [9]

And Professor Toynbee, describing some of the descendants of these colonial sluggards, finds that "the Appalachian 'mountain people' today are no better than barbarians. They have relapsed into illiteracy and witchcraft. They suffer from poverty, squalor and ill-health. They are the American counterparts of the latter-day white barbarians of the Old World—Riffs, Albanians, Kurds, Pathans, and Hairy Ainus; but whereas these latter are belated survivals of an ancient barbarism, the Appalachians present the melancholy spectacle of a people who have acquired civilization and then lost it." [10] Describing the barbarizing influence of the American frontier, Toynbee quotes the most famous of the historians of the frontier, Frederick Jackson Turner, in support of his ideas about the "spiritual malady of barbarization" in frontier societies.

But both Turner and Toynbee discount or overlook the potent minority of culture bearers who plant and cultivate the elements of traditional civilization on each successive frontier. That was the significance of the planters of the Chesapeake Bay region. These men exerted such a powerful influence and established such a vital civilization, albeit a rural society, that their ideas and concepts dominated a great region for the generations which followed them. The English tradition was so thoroughly established that the South has remained the section of the United States most sympathetic to Britain and things British.

While the Chesapeake Bay agrarians were establishing a picket line of English civilization along their waterways, New Englanders were organizing towns and reproducing the kind of traditional culture which their religion and their mores dictated. Because geographical conditions favored trade and commerce instead of an exclusively agrarian economy, New England became a region of villages and towns instead of a commonwealth of scattered plantations. The mere physical fact of grouping in close communities made the struggle against barbarism much simpler in New England than in the South. Furthermore, many of the New England settlers came as closely knit groups with definite ideas of the kind of society which they proposed to establish. They were simply transferring to what they hoped would be a more favorable environment a religious and social culture which they were determined to defend with all of the resources at their command.

Puritanism, which in some variety predominated throughout New England, was a militant faith, full of vigor and strength. The force and energy of the Puritans' determination to civilize whatever land they occupied affected the whole later course of American history. Whether the Puritans were operating in Boston in 1635 or in San Francisco in 1849, they made their influence felt. The godless trembled and the ignorant soon found themselves being instructed. No Puritan was ever willing to tolerate either devil or dunce.

Although seventeenth-century Puritans had no monopoly of piety and moral rectitude, they practiced more intensely than others certain austere and prudential virtues which coincided with the ideals of the rising middle class. We do not have to agree entirely with Max Weber's famous thesis on capitalism and the Protestant ethic to concede that the Puritan code of behavior was highly effective in developing the doctrine of success which has become a part of the American social dogma. The Puritans were not the only ones who taught the virtues of diligence, thrift, and sobriety, but they emphasized these qualities to such a degree that extravagance became a cardinal sin and work was regarded as a worthy end in itself. Having forsworn waste of either time or money, and having made a virtue of unceasing diligence in his calling, a Puritan, unless he had phenomenally bad luck, could hardly escape material success. Furthermore, he devised an educational system intended to sharpen his wits and make his mind a more effective instrument for dealing with his fellow men. It is small wonder that the Yankee in the nineteenth century became a byword for resourcefulness and shrewdness. Actually he represented the ultimate flowering of the seventeenth-century middle class who were strongly Puritan in their backgrounds.

The political doctrine of Manifest Destiny which played such an important part in westward expansion was a natural outgrowth of the Puritan belief that they were God's chosen people. New Englanders, whether in the seventeenth century or in later periods, have always had a strong conviction of their divine calling to "improve" the world. From the beginning in this country they have been inspired apostles of their particular civilization, and wherever they have gone, from Massachusetts to Ohio and thence to the Pacific Coast, they have displayed a zeal for religion, learning, and social improvement in accordance with their traditional ideas. If we cannot credit Puritan New Englanders with the entire responsibility for civilizing the West, we can discern evidence of their intense activity in nearly every locality. They were a busy and convinced social group, intent upon reproducing their society wherever they went. In most places they succeeded, sometimes too well.

Nothing so clearly illustrates the Puritan determination to reproduce the best of the civilization they had known as their zeal for education. The founding of Harvard College in 1636, only a few years after the first settlements in Massachusetts Bay, is indicative of a crusading attitude toward learning which would endure from that day to this. An often-quoted passage from *New Englands First Fruits* (1643) is worth repeating because it sums up so much of the Puritan attitude: "After God had carried us safe to New England, and wee had builded our houses, provided necessaries for our livelihood, reared convenient places for Gods worship, and setled the Civill Government: One of the next things we longed for, and looked after was to advance Learning and Perpetuate it to Posterity; dreading to leave an illiterate Ministery to the Churches, when our present Ministers shall lie in the Dust. And as wee were thinking and consulting how to effect this great Work; it pleased God to stir up the heart of one Mr. Harvard (a godly Gentleman and lover of Learning, there living amongst us) to give the one halfe of his Estate (it being in all about £1700) towards the erecting of a Colledge: and all his Library: after him another gave £300 others after them cast in more, and the publique hand of the State added the rest: the Colledge was, by common consent, appointed to be at Cambridge, (a place very pleasing and accommodate) and is called (according to the name of the first founder) Harvard Colledge." [11]

The very essence of Protestantism was the doctrine that every individual had a right and obligation to read the Scriptures, and it followed that if he read the

Scriptures he had the privilege of drawing his own conclusions about the meaning. Now the Puritans were not a sentimental and soft-headed folk, and they did not subscribe to the notion that interpretation of the Scriptures by anybody, regardless of education, was equally valid. Consequently they were at pains to provide institutions which could supply them with a learned clergy and also assure a laity sufficiently educated to make the most of their religious opportunities. The founding of schools and colleges therefore took on a high religious motive which transcended mere social service. Wherever the Puritans and their descendants have gone, from 1636 to our own day, they have furnished leaders dedicated to education, and their migrations across the continent can be traced by their schoolhouses and their colleges, monuments to a religious ideal. Perhaps the Puritans' most important and most enduring contribution to American society has been a persistent zeal for learning and their equation of religion with education.

So well did the Puritans transplant their culture to New England that some of their colleagues who had remained at home sent their sons to Harvard to drink from a purer fountain than could be found at Oxford and Cambridge during the troublous years of the midseventeenth century. Puritan preachers who went out from Harvard, and later, from Yale and other colleges, became great teachers and civilizers of frontier communities. When Puritan communities migrated and established new towns in the Connecticut Valley, or farther westward, the pastor was usually the leader and he and his elders saw to it that the new town reproduced the characteristics of a civilized society as they knew it.

Occasionally Puritan communities went very far afield indeed, as when in 1695 a congregation from Dorchester, Massachusetts, moved to South Carolina and settled a new southern Dorchester. But they carried their traditional beliefs and qualities and re-established them under the warmer South Carolina sun. To save them from the corruption of semitropical ease and Anglican latitudinarianism, Cotton Mather supplied them copiously with sermons of his own composition. Within a few years, the citizens of Dorchester, S. C., procured the passage of an act in the Assembly establishing an elementary school with a provision, however, for the teaching of Latin and Greek. They did not intend to let their children grow up barbarous in the swamps of South Carolina.

The repetition in new communities of the older civilization was of concern to those who remained in the parent hive as well as to the migrants who left. In a letter of instructions, written in 1697 to a group of settlers who went out from Essex County, Massachusetts, to South Carolina, the writer gives some prudent advice: "We do pray and request," he urges, "that you endeavor (and let God help you) to carry and behave yourselves as good and sober men, which we hope you will, and that you will not err from your former conversation, which we have observed to be adorned with

prudence and sobriety. Indeed we do rather propose
this caution, in that we have been informed that many
of New England going into that country have so de-
meaned themselves as that they have been a scandal
to New England and have been an offence to the sober
and well minded in Carolina and an ill example unto
others. Therefore we pray you will remember you are
in this voyage concerned not only for a worldly interest
but (though remotely yet really) for the translating
Christ's ordinances and worship into that country.
Therefore honor God, your [blank in Ms], and your
persons by good behavior." [12]

Wherever they went, the Puritans took with them
books, not merely pious books, but the basis of humane
letters. Even the Separatists who settled Plymouth,
most of whom would not be considered learned men,
brought along little libraries of surprising diversity.
William Brewster, for example, included among his
books Machiavelli's *Prince*, Sir Thomas Smith's *The
Commonwealth of England and Manner of Government*, Richard Knolles' translation from Bodin, *The Six
Books of a Commonwealth*, the *Civil Conversations*, a
sort of Emily Post handbook by Stephano Guazzo, and
a copy of *A Help to Memory and Discourse*, a manual
designed to prevent one's conversation from becoming
rude and provincial.

The influence of some of the small private libraries
which the New Englanders brought with them and
collected after their arrival was incalculable, for they
were in effect circulating libraries. John Winthrop, Jr.,

who became governor of the Connecticut colony, brought a diversified collection of books, including many scientific works. From the time of his arrival in 1631 until his death in 1676, his library was freely used by neighbors and friends. One of these, Jonathan Brewster, read so many books on alchemy that his mind became muddled. Another friend of Winthrop's, Gershom Bulkeley, better balanced than Brewster, read with such discrimination that his tombstone declared him to have been "exquisite in his skill in divinity, physic, and law, and of a most exemplary Christian life." [13] He collected scientific books himself and stimulated scientific observation. In fact, the Puritan interest in science was keen, and even in what then were remote communities, men were keeping up with the discussions in the Royal Society and sometimes contributing their bits of scientific observation. The fact that they lived in compact villages and towns made communication and the exchange of books easy.

But no outpost was too distant to be altogether lacking in reading matter. Boston early had booksellers who supplied the outlying regions. Hezekiah Usher, a merchant, as early as 1642 opened a bookshop in Boston and by 1700 Boston had at least seven booksellers. Other more distant towns also had merchants who sold books as part of their regular stock in trade. Furthermore, peddlers carried books and pamphlets to the very fringes of the wilderness. Cotton Mather realized the civilizing value of the books distributed by peddlers, as an entry in his diary for June 11, 1683, indicates: "There is an old hawker, who will fill this country with devout and useful books if I will direct him. I therefore will direct him, and assist him, as far as I can in doing this." [14] Apparently the peddlers succeeded too well as distributers of literature not precisely to Mather's liking, for he commented a few years later: "I am informed that the minds and manners of many people about the country are much corrupted by foolish songs and ballads which the hawkers and peddlers carry into all parts of the country. By way of antidote, I would procure poetical composures full of piety and such as may have a tendency to advance truth and goodness to be published and scattered into all corners of the land. There may be an extract of some from the excellent Watts's hymns." [15] Mather was keenly aware of the influence of books and was anxious to persuade the booksellers to bring in the right sort of literature, books, as he said in one place, to "serve the interests of truth and piety."

If a Puritan pioneer could take with him no other book, he wanted at least a Bible, which provided him with a whole literature as well as a guide to life. When John Sandbrooke, servant of John Winthrop, in 1638 found that he was to stay ten months on the Isle of Sables with a sealing party he wrote back earnestly requesting "a Bible, a quire of paper, and some sealing wax." [16] Though he thanked God that his stomach could "digest seals, gulls, foxes, owl, and such meat as the Lord is pleased to provide" his spirit could not endure the desolation of the Isle of Sables without a Bible to guide, instruct, console, and entertain him.

The civilizing influence of this one book was incalculable. The English Bible was something more than a religious talisman, a holy book. It was the basis of religious doctrine, to be sure, but the Puritan believed that it also contained the sum of wisdom on every other subject. He read the Bible diligently, quoted it on all occasions, and unconsciously absorbed the rhythms of its prose, its metaphors, and its style. Frontiersmen from John Sandbrooke to Abraham Lincoln owed a great deal more to the Bible than they perhaps realized.

Other religious sects paralleled the New England Puritans in their zeal to maintain the elements of traditional civilization in the backwoods. Indeed, the most notable contribution in the second half of the colonial period was made by Scotch-Irish Presbyterians, chiefly Scots from Northern Ireland. After the turn of the eighteenth century, they poured into America, principally through the port of Philadelphia, though some entered at Charleston, South Carolina, and at other ports. Pushing past the older settlements, they made their way to the back country and fanned out down the river valleys of Pennsylvania and moved on into adjacent territory. They became the typical frontiersmen of the period, the spearheads of white penetration of Indian territory.

The Scots brought with them a deep-seated hatred

for the English who had tried to make them conform to the Established Church and had imposed economic restrictions which had hindered their efforts to make a livelihood in Ulster. Bearing a grudge already against the political order which they had known, they were natural revolutionaries and became notable agitators against the English during the prelude to the American Revolution.

But culturally these Scots were exceedingly conservative. They were convinced that the Presbyterian form of church government was the best and that the religious dogma expounded by John Knox was the surest—if not the only—way to salvation. They also had a profound respect for learning, especially classical learning, and their ministers were carriers of this tradition wherever they went. A tough-minded and serious people, they made the establishment of the traditional kirk a concern second only to the elemental needs of food and shelter. Immediately after the erection of churches came the establishment of schools. Long before the American Revolution, the Scots had established a chain of Presbyterian churches and schools along the frontier from New England to Georgia. These fortresses against ignorance and the devil paralleled a chain of blockhouses and forts against the French and Indian.[17] The Scots were as eager to fight one as the other.

Preachers accompanied the settlers into the wilderness and clergymen who held degrees from the University of Edinburgh, and later from Princeton, lived in the same kind of log cabin as those occupied by their far-flung parishioners. These pioneer parsons rode horseback from clearing to clearing, teaching and preaching as they went. They were a fearless group who exerted an enormous influence over their people. Not only were the preachers spiritual guides but they also frequently served as civil and military leaders as well. One of the most famous of the soldier-preachers was the Reverend John Elder, pastor of the church at Derry, Pennsylvania, from 1738 to 1791. Commissioned a captain by the Pennsylvania government, he led a company of rangers and was accustomed to preach with his loaded musket across the pulpit. A graduate of Edinburgh, Elder was a classical scholar equally at home tracing the wanderings of Ulysses or tracking down the most recent Indian marauder.

These hard-riding, long-winded preachers of the Presbyterian faith were the apostles of both religion and learning. They insisted that every child should know at least enough to read the Bible and the Shorter Catechism. They distributed books and tracts. And they taught the children as well as their parents. They were instrumental in stirring up backward settlements to establish neighborhood schools, and they persuaded itinerant schoolmasters to make their way around the circuits which the preachers rode.

Like the Puritans of New England and the Anglicans of Virginia, the Scotch-Irish Presbyterians were concerned lest the supply of learned preachers and teachers fail, and to that end they established academies and colleges to train ministers and laymen. Their first institution of higher learning was the famous "Log College," founded about 1726 by the Reverend William Tennent, Sr. at Neshaminy, Pennsylvania. Tennent, who received his own education at Edinburgh, was skillful in Latin and the other learned languages and his academy taught Latin, Greek, logic, rhetoric, and theology. When George Whitefield, the evangelist, visited the academy in 1739, he reported that "seven or eight worthy ministers of Jesus have lately been sent forth; more are almost ready to be sent, and a foundation is now laying for the instruction of many others." [18] John Blair and Samuel Finley, early presidents of Princeton, were graduates of this frontier academy. The establishment of Princeton in 1746 was inspired by the need of insuring a learned Presbyterian clergy, but the founders provided a broad base of learning and opened the doors to men of all faiths.[19] From Princeton went scores of preachers and teachers to frontier settlements to keep alive the germ of classical culture.

The Scotch Presbyterians on the frontier showed a continuing zeal for the founding of schools and the perpetuation of traditional learning. The maintenance of churches and schools imposed considerable hardships upon a people who had little ready money. For a major portion of their subsistence preachers and teachers could not expect cash but had to accept payment in the products of the country. As tobacco was a medium of exchange in Virginia in the seventeenth century, so whisky became one of the most convenient of assets on the western frontier in the eighteenth. Preachers and teachers were not averse to accepting jugs of rye and corn whisky as contributions toward their upkeep. The Scots who had introduced the art and mystery of distilling whisky from rye and corn mash saw nothing incongruous in devoting a portion of their honored product to the advancement of spiritual and intellectual salvation.

Struggle as colonial Americans might to retain the cultivation of the mother country, they sometimes found themselves fighting a losing battle. The hardships of the wilderness were too great to leave much time for anything except the bitter struggle for survival. The second generation of Americans, even in such literate spots as Boston, appeared to be less cultivated than their elders, but perhaps, as Professor Samuel Eliot Morison has suggested, they merely reflected a prosaic period.[20] A significant fact is that colonial Americans themselves were so conscious of their loss from the dimming of the cultural lamps that they were eternally trying to improve the sources of illumination.

The desire for self-improvement has been one of the most characteristic qualities in Americans from the earliest times to the present day. One has only to read the advertisements of correspondence courses and manuals for self-help in our periodicals to realize how widespread is that appeal today. Benjamin Franklin's *Autobiography* gives a vivid account of the procedure by which one of the greatest colonials educated himself and made himself proficient in the useful knowledge of the past. Franklin is an excellent example of the transmission of ideas from the Old World to the New, for much of his pragmatic philosophy which has so profoundly influenced American thinking had its origin in the ideas of the English middle class of the late sixteenth and early seventeenth centuries.[21]

One of the works that influenced Franklin was *The Spectator* which he read and deliberately imitated. Franklin was not the only American who found the works of Joseph Addison and Richard Steele both entertaining and improving. Few English authors had greater influence upon eighteenth-century Americans than these two, and the reason is not hard to find. Addison and Steele provided sound and "improving" reading matter designed to teach good manners, decorum, decency, and urbanity with the least possible pain to the reader. Their ideas coincided with the common-sense, middle-class notions which dominated most American thinking, whether of the agrarian aristocracy or the trading classes in such centers as Boston and Philadelphia. Implicit in *The Spectator* was the ideal of self-improvement which appealed especially to colonial Americans and became a part of our social dogma.

The Spectator was, of course, only one of many influences which helped to shape second and third generation Americans into the mold of civilized Englishmen. The conscious effort to reproduce English society succeeded almost too well in certain areas. Charleston, South Carolina, for example, did its best to be a replica of London in little and imitated the good as well as the bad qualities of the British capital. Many Charlestonians went to London for business and professional reasons and brought back manners, habits, and customs of the metropolis. Many others imported the current books and periodicals which gave them an insight into the civilized world across the Atlantic.

In all the urban centers in colonial America the same thing was happening. For all of its polyglot population, Philadelphia, the largest of the American towns at the end of the colonial period—and the second city in the British empire—became a center of British culture. That is not to say that German and French influences were invisible, or that Quaker Philadelphians were like Anglican Charlestonians, but that the most important influences at work in that society were English, and London was the focal point from which Philadelphians imported ideas. From the towns and cities along the seaboard, the elements of civilization percolated to the most distant frontiers. Long before the end of the colonial period, British culture was already penetrating the rudest settlements to the west.

TWO

Enlightenment in the Old West: The Kentucky Borderland

L ONG before the thirteen colonies had won
their independence from Great Britain, pioneers had crossed the mountain barrier and had penetrated what to them was the Far West. Though the
government in London might run a Proclamation Line
along the crest of the Alleghenies in 1763 and decree
that the land beyond was sacred to the Indians and
the fur trade, the laws of London were of no avail
against the land hunger of Virginians, Pennsylvanians,
or New Englanders willing to risk their scalps for the
sake of holdings in the rich valleys of rivers that
flowed to the West. After the Revolution, of course, a
horde of settlers swept over the mountains. Sporadic
Indian forays might slaughter a few and frighten the
timid, but immigrants pressed on. Our first soldiers'
bonus was paid in warrants entitling veterans of the
Revolution to western lands. The question of jurisdiction over these lands was one of the most critical problems affecting the young nation, and the cession of
western territory claimed by the Atlantic states required delicate diplomacy in the early days of the
Republic. In a series of ordinances during the period

of the Confederation, Congress brought some order out of the chaos and paved the way for the transmission of the Atlantic civilization to the Old West, the region between the Alleghenies and the Mississippi.

The early migrations focussed upon lands of the central region of the Old West, upon Tennessee and Kentucky in what was known as the Southwest Territory, and upon Ohio and, a little later, upon Indiana and Illinois in the Northwest Territory.

Very early, land speculation became a characteristic of American business life, a characteristic that we have retained to the present day. The real estate promoter is not a modern invention, even though he may have thought up some new angles in our time. Before the Revolution, speculators were appraising their opportunities for profit in western land, and after the war with England had opened up the region beyond the mountains, real estate promotion became an obsession with business men who dreamed of quick riches to be made in the West. Land companies sprouted and grew overnight. With vague maps before them, promoters sold farms and homesites in a wilderness they had never seen.

The story of the land companies is so involved and devious that the modern student becomes almost as confused as the purchasers of land must have been in the 1790's. The speculators themselves were often doubtful of the precise location of the lands which they had purchased or obtained on options from the government. Joel Barlow, the poet, agent for the Scioto Company in

Paris in 1788, in all innocence sold farms between the Scioto and Ohio rivers which later turned out to belong to the Ohio Company of Associates. Approximately six hundred French artisans, craftsmen, and other non-farmers, persuaded by the seductive prospectus, invested in American prosperity. On October 17, 1790, they arrived at an Ohio swamp and settled in a village of log huts which took the name of Gallipolis. Such of the unhappy Frenchmen who persisted in staying eventually paid the Ohio Company $1.25 an acre for land which they had already bought in Paris, and ultimately they were assimilated in the Anglo-Saxon society which enveloped them. Although fraud was perhaps not characteristic of the dealings of the early land companies, the opportunities for quick riches were so great that all sorts of shady speculators hawked prospectuses and the simple farmer in search of fresh land had to be wary indeed.

From the beginning, the West has had an irresistible appeal. Always over the horizon toward the setting sun lay opportunity. The Spanish conquistadors endured incredible hardships in search of the golden Seven Cities of Cíbola. Fur traders, French and British, always believed that the river, just beyond where they were, would yield a bountiful return in beaver or otter the like of which they had not yet known. Eastern farmers on rocky acres in New England or on burned-out tobacco farms in Virginia and Maryland dreamed of black alluvial soil across the mountains where crops would produce seven-fold and they might multiply their holdings of property. So great was the appeal of the West that men and women were ready to risk their lives to claim a part of the land across the Alleghenies. The Indians might make trouble for a time, but, inevitably as the tide, the white torrent would sweep over them and push them back like driftwood into the far corners of the land.

The lure of the West would become an influence affecting every Eastern household for generations to come. Boys hearing tales of Indian fighting or bear-hunting in the forests of Kentucky would treasure the memory and plan to go West as soon as they were old enough. Tenant farmers, tired of paying a part of their labor to landlords, would look into the sunset toward lands which they might hope to own in fee simple and be masters of their own fates. Landed proprietors, surveying their restricted holdings and counting their numerous progeny, saw in the West opportunities to obtain sufficient land to establish all of their sons and daughters as substantial people of property. Ambitious lawyers and politicians knew that they might get ahead faster in the West. Rascals and ne'er-do-wells thought their chances of flourishing were greater if they escaped the trammels of settled existence in the East. Men and women of every type and description, the prosperous and the poor, the educated and the unlearned, the pious and the godless, all would look to the West with varying degrees of yearning. But the majority of the migrants to the West consisted of the ambitious but respectable poor, eager to find greater prosperity in a new country. There were also many who went out of a spirit of restless adventure.

Wherever they went, life at first was hard, and the struggle for survival against the forces of elemental nature and the neolithic red man repeated the experiences of colonial settlers on the Atlantic frontier. The Anglo-Saxon had held a foothold in the East now for nearly two centuries and the wilderness had taught him something, if not much. At any rate, most of the settlers who crossed the mountains were better prepared for a frontier existence than the first immigrants had been. Yet no amount of inherited experience could mitigate the hardships of frontier life. The basic conditions of the forest, the land, and the Indians were the same, and in some fashion those intractable elements had to be conquered before the settlers could reap the rewards of peace and plenty in their new homes. They had little time for the softer pursuits of life, for letters and learning, even if they had the inclination. For them, the axe, the hoe, the plow, and the rifle had to take precedence over book and pen. The struggle between the powers of darkness and the angels of light for the soul and mind of the pioneer was just as critical as it had been in the earlier period. In some respects the advantage now lay with the adversary, for many of the transmontane pioneers carried less cultural equipment than their forefathers had possessed. Daniel Boone is remembered as the prototype of the pioneer, and no one has recorded that he was a bookish man, though he is said to have dictated his autobiography to John Filson, who published it in 1784 in *The Discovery, Settlement And present State of Kentucke.* Indeed, the early biographers of Boone described with considerable relish the fact that the youth put ipecac in his Irish schoolmaster's whisky, knocked him down when he objected, and left school at an early age.

The quality of the average pioneer is described by Daniel Drake, who as a child in the summer on 1788 emigrated with his family from New Jersey to Mayslick, Kentucky. Most of the group were East and West Jersey people but there were others:

The immigrants from other states were almost entirely Virginians and Marylanders. All were country people by birth and residence—all were illiterate, but in various degrees—& all were poor, or in moderate circumstances—a majority or, a least, a moiety, however, were small freeholders. As to religious and moral refinement & a knowledge and use of the domestic arts of civilized life, the Jersey emigrants, as a body, were superior. Next came the Virginians, and last and lowest, the Marylanders; who, in many respects, were not equal to the Kentucky negroes of the *present* day. Of such was my old *domine,* Master Beaden. . . .[1]

All the first settlers of Mays Lick were, either by association or profession, Baptists, and had belonged to the church at Scotch Plains. . . . At what time after their immigration a house of public worship was erected, I do not remember, but recollect to have attended public worship in Mr. Morris' barn. It happened that most of the Jersey & Virginia families, around the village, were likewise Baptists, & therefore it was the predominant sect. . . .[2]

It may be interesting to you to know something of the

Baptist preachers and the prevalent religious ideas of those days. Most of the former were illiterate persons, but some were men of considerable natural talents. They all lacked dignity & solemnity, and some of them now & then uttered very droll expressions in the pulpit. This was the case with several brothers by the name of Craig, emigrants from Virginia, whose descendants are extensively spread over the state of Kentucky. . . .[3]

Presbyterian ministers occasionally preached in the village; but found little favour with the (predominant) Baptist people. The objections to them, as I well recollect were their advocacy of sprinkling & of infant baptism, and their having been educated in early life to the ministry as to a profession. The Methodists were, on the main, Marylanders and Virginians—the former predominating. Most of them were among the lamentably ignorant. . . . Throughout the whole period of my residence there, I never knew a single Episcopalian.[4]

These settlers had small cultural attainments. Some were even suspicious of book learning and looked with disfavor upon the Presbyterian ministers who represented a type of learning which their own Baptist and Methodist preachers might consider a spiritual liability. Yet these semi-literate country people were not devoid of ambition to improve their cultural status, or at least to see that their children had better opportunities than had been their own fortune. Some of them, to be sure, were content to remain in sodden ignorance; some thought schooling would merely waste their children's time and take their minds off the proper business of hunting, trapping, or farming; but most wanted something better for their boys and girls. Frontier communities established old field schools, hired such school-masters as they could find, and trusted that their children would learn the rudiments of reading, writing, and arithmetic, for these were the foundations of civilized life. They might even provide a step toward one of the learned professions. If a son could become a lawyer or a doctor, that was a mark not only of professional success but of cultural advancement.

The very fact that Daniel Drake who wrote the account of pioneer days in Kentucky, the son of semiliterate parents, could rise to such eminence that he became known as the "Franklin of the West" is not merely proof that genius transcends environment but that the milieu itself was not utterly lacking in opportunity. Drake's background was unpromising. Describing his family, he observes that both his father and mother "could read and write, though neither of them knew any thing of grammar, geography or arithmetic. Their reading could not have been extensive, for when I could first remember, the Bible, Rippon's Collection of hymns, the almanac, Dilworth's Spelling book, and a romance of the ages of Chivalry, entitled the *'Famous history of Montellion'* made up their whole library. The [last] I should greatly like to see again." [5] Advocates today of the "great books" would not consider this an adequate library, but these books at least provided the elemental basis of self-education. "During my boyhood," Drake continues, "there was in the country (except among wealthy emigrants from Old Virginia of whom, however, there were none about Mayslick) a great deficiency of books. There was not a single book store north of Licking River and, perhaps, none in the state. All the books imported were kept in what were called *Stores* which were magazines of the most primitive character . . . Bibles, hymn books, primers, spelling books, arithmetics & almanacs, in fact composed, in most instances, the importation." [6]

In some fashion the youngster, like other bright boys on the frontier, acquired a few books that stirred his imagination and his taste for learning. When he was twelve or thirteen, his father bought from a neighbor a book on surveying which gave him his first knowledge of geometry. William Guthrie's *Geographical, Historical, and Commercial Grammar* (1770), Noah Webster's blue-back spelling book, a pocket dictionary, an anthology of pieces for recitation, Aesop's *Fables,* Bunyan's *Pilgrim's Progress,* Franklin's *Autobiography,* John Dickinson's *Letters from a Farmer in Pennsylvania to the Inhabitants of the British Colonies* (1768), and an occasional copy of the *Kentucky Gazette*[7] together with the inherited Bible, hymn books, and *Montelion,* constituted Drake's introduction to literary learning before he went off to Cincinnati at the age of fifteen to become an apprentice in medicine to Dr. William Goforth.

Not the size of a library, nor the care with which the books are selected, is a guarantee of their influence on the reader. In Drake's case he had few books, but those few made a profound impression upon him. For example, he comments about his reading of *Pilgrim's Progress* that "although it was declared to be a dream, all the characters became to me as real personages—as real as if they had been dramatis personae acting before me." [8] Like Benjamin Franklin he made the most of scanty opportunities. While apprenticed to Dr. Goforth he learned Latin. He continued his studies, and his inquiring mind made him in time the most distinguished scientist in the West, the author of several important books, including a classic work on the diseases of the Mississippi Valley, the founder of schools, libraries, and learned institutions, and an intellectual leader in his region.

The mass of the immigrants who poured into the West were undoubtedly as culturally deficient as the group whom Drake described but there were others too. Some well-to-do citizens of Virginia brought something besides silver cups for mint juleps. They had books and notions of a cultivated life which they translated to Kentucky or Ohio. From North Carolina and Pennsylvania came hard-bitten Scotch Presbyterians who listened to their dominies quote Latin and John Knox and hoped that at least some of their children might acquire learning enough to become ministers or lawyers. From New England came a group conditioned to the custom of maintaining township schools and providing systematically for public education. They equated piety with learning and believed that schools would show the way to salvation. To the New England immigrants, especially in Ohio, has been attributed much of the zeal for education on that frontier, but careful surveys of the population and their cultural activities indicate that no single group can be given the major credit.[9] Cultural developments in the Old West represent an amalgam of a wide variety of influences.

We have become accustomed to thinking of the Ohio and Mississippi river frontiers in the early days as dominated by roistering river boatmen, rowdies who broke up Methodist camp meetings, or bullies who fought with knives and never left a fight without gouging out their opponent's eye or biting off his ear. We remember the characters of folklore who boasted of being half-horse, half-alligator, ready to wrestle a wildcat or ride a bolt of lightning. Such is the stuff of colorful fiction, some of it contemporary with the days of settlement. But we forget prosaic schoolteachers and preachers, as well as the earnest and decent citizens, determined to make a better life for themselves and their families with all of the appurtenances of civilization.

The individualistic emigrants from Virginia, Maryland, New Jersey, Pennsylvania, and the Carolinas who first settled Kentucky had no conventionalized pattern of village schools such as the New Englanders brought with them, but in their hit-or-miss fashion they provided some sort of education for their children, hiring a schoolmaster when they could find one, good, bad, or indifferent, and setting up schools in cabins, barns, or brush arbors. Many a prominent citizen of the state could remember no formal schooling beyond that which he received from some itinerant Scot or wandering Yankee schoolmaster who tarried for a while in the neighborhood and instructed the children in the rudiments of reading and arithmetic.

One of the first schoolmasters in Kentucky was John Filson, who had received his own education at the hands of the Reverend Samuel Finley, later president of Princeton. Filson taught a school in Lexington probably as early as 1782, dabbled in land, and wrote *The Discovery, Settlement And present State of Kentucke* (Wilmington, 1784), as a prospectus to attract land buyers. In 1788 he was advertising in the *Kentucky Gazette* a seminary which would give a liberal education, including a knowledge of the French language, and improve the manners and morals of its students. Unhappily Filson was killed that same year by an Indian, and his praiseworthy academy never developed. But his proposal was typical of schools which served their announced purpose of ministering to both the intellectual and spiritual needs of their students. The *Kentucky Gazette*, for example, published a notice on December 27, 1787, that Messrs. Jones and Worley would open a school "at the royal spring in Lebanon town, Fayette county, where a commodious house, sufficient to contain fifty or sixty scholars, will be prepared. They will teach the Latin and Greek languages, together with such branches of the sciences as are generally taught in public seminaries, at twenty-five shillings a quarter for each scholar, one half to be paid in cash, the other in produce at cash price." [10] Before the war whoops of the Indians had ceased echoing in the woods on each side of the Ohio, little academies for the transmission of the classical tradition were already in operation. Within a few years after clearings were made in the forests, the language and literature of Greece and Rome were available to youths of Kentucky and Ohio. Traditional civilization, transplanted to new soil, would flourish amazingly.

This is not to imply that frontiersmen of the Old West lapsed into Latin and spent such idle hours as they could find reading Plato in Greek. The mass of the people, then as now, devoted their time to less edifying if more practical pursuits. But the germ of the old culture was very much alive and would spread throughout the body of western society. The leaders in these western communities were as much concerned as their colonial predecessors had been lest their children grow up barbarous in the wilderness. Their methods of circumventing barbarism varied in accordance with their backgrounds and geographical origins, but regardless of whether the pioneers came from the more relaxed South or the sterner North, they took steps to provide some of the instruments of civilization.

Not all af the pioneers, it must be admitted, were profoundly concerned with cultural matters. The frontier from the beginning saw a sharp division between the apostles of traditional culture and the scoffers and scorners. At the lowest level, some of the illiterate looked upon "book larnin' " as an invention of the devil to plague or mislead honest folk who could more profitably spend their spare time bear-hunting, attending a corn-shucking, or listening to the warnings of a revivalist at the annual camp meeting. Others somewhat higher in the intellectual scale were also skeptical of too much fancy learning and argued that Westerners needed practical education. Reading, arithmetic, and surveying would be good for anybody, but beyond that, well, one had to be careful not to waste too much time and money on frills. Opposed to these were substantial numbers who wanted for the West as good cultural opportunities as the East had ever offered. The conflict between these points of view would rage in American community life on each successive frontier, and would persist as a dominant factor in American education until our own day. A significant fact often overlooked, however, is the degree of success achieved by traditionalists who were prevailingly a numerical minority.

The early history of Kentucky is instructive, for, as we have seen, it was settled by a motley horde of emigrants chiefly from the Southern and Middle colonies. Between 1783 and 1790, the date of the first Federal census, the population of Kentucky expanded from approximately 12,000 to 70,000. To these settlers education had been a matter of individual concern. They had no tradition of public schools or government support for secondary education. But the reproduction of a civilized way of life meant some degree of schooling even in the opinion of simple folk like Daniel Drake's parents, and very early the question of the kind and quality of education became a subject of vigorous controversy.

A distinguished historian of Kentucky, surveying the

educational history of that region, thinks the pioneers were slow in transferring eastern institutions, but despite their inattention to formal education, "they brought with them the idea that to allow a man to reach maturity without being able to read was abomination in the sight of God," and they saw to it that "all the forts had crude schools taught by some literate member of the community." [11]

Schoolmasters of various kinds, Scots, Irishmen, Yankees, and Frenchmen, swarmed into Kentucky in the two decades before 1800, and set up schools which claimed to teach most of the known subjects including such accomplishments as dancing, fencing, painting, and music. Schooling at first was entirely in the hands of private teachers and, in some instances, of preachers of the various religious sects. A Kentucky citizen complained in 1787 because "every neighborhood encourages schools under different teachers according to prevailing doctrines" and selfish interests dominate education.[12] The Kentucky frontier had its share of rationalists and Jeffersonian republicans who feared any religious domination of education, and it was natural that they would support an agitation for secular schools supported by public funds.

By 1798, the legislature of the young state of Kentucky had passed two acts providing for county academies supported from public lands, 6,000 acres to each school. The counties could also conduct lotteries to defray the initial expenses of the schools. But though public education became a subject of violent political controversy from this time onward, the county academies made small headway against the private schools, partly because of the neglect of local trustees and partly because the school land was insufficient to support them.[13] The important fact to remember, however, is that education supported in part at public expense was of sufficient concern to a large number of frontier citizens to make it a live political issue throughout the early history of the state.

While Kentucky was still a frontier region it saw the establishment of one of the most remarkable institutions of classical learning in the country, and certainly the most remarkable institution in the West for many years to come. This was Transylvania University at Lexington. In 1780 when Kentucky was a county of Virginia that commonwealth appropriated 8,000 acres of land formerly belonging to Kentucky Tories to found a public school "to promote the diffusion of knowledge even amongst the most remote citizens whose situation, a barbarous neighborhood and savage intercourse, might otherwise render unfriendly to science." [14] Transylvania Seminary, as it was first called, opened in 1785 in the Lincoln County home of a learned Presbyterian divine, the Reverend David Rice, a Princeton graduate. A few years later the school moved to Lexington and in 1794 the trustees chose Harry Toulmin, a Baptist, president. This was too much for the Presbyterians who had nursed the little academy along, and they withdrew and established Kentucky Academy at Pisgah in Woodford County. Eventually, on December 22, 1798, the two academies were consolidated as Transylvania University.[15]

Besides its liberal arts college, Transylvania had a school of law and a school of medicine. It drew to its faculty distinguished scholars and scientists, and it developed an excellent library. In the first quarter of the nineteenth century it was one of the most liberal institutions in the nation. During its period of greatest development, from 1818 to 1827, it had for its president Horace Holley, a graduate of Yale, but a Unitarian without the conservatism which characterized many of Yale's Congregational graduates who went West to teach and establish schools.

Combining classical learning with the new spirit of scientific inquiry, Transylvania for a time was a brilliant example of the best in the humanistic tradition. Political liberals of the Jeffersonian variety and intellectuals intent upon freeing the human mind of the shackles of ancient dogma looked upon Transylvania as a beacon light of freedom. Naturally it aroused the antagonism of reactionaries. The frontier, for all of its reputed freedom from conventions, has always had a large and vocal group intent upon rooting out heresies, especially intellectual heresies. Transylvania quickly became the target of disgruntled Presbyterians who had lost control of it, of reactionaries who believed it to be tainted with French Jacobinism (the equivalent of a charge of Communism today), and of many others who always suspected higher learning of encouraging general iniquity. The outlines of the attack on learning, familiar today in the loose charges brought against colleges, universities, and foundations of harboring and encouraging subversives, may be seen in the charges against Transylvania, an institution too advanced for its milieu.

So great was the hostility of the more orthodox that the Associated Reformed Presbyterians preferred charges against a Scottish minister of their sect, Robert Hamilton Bishop, who had accepted a professorship in Transylvania University without the presbytery's permission. In his reply to the charges, Bishop defended not only himself but the university against enemies who opposed its secular freedom from domination by any group. Its purpose, he declared, was to "disseminate over these Western countries *that knowledge,* and *only that knowledge,* which all reasonable [men] of whatever denomination unite in acknowledging to be of the last importance, for the good of both civil and religious society. In accomplishing this great end she knows neither sect, nor party, whether religious or political." [16] But the enemies of liberal learning were too numerous and Transylvania's great days were numbered. Bishop, who had made such a strong defense of the institution, left in 1824 to become president of Miami University at Oxford, Ohio, and Holley himself resigned in 1827 and took boat for New Orleans. Transylvania did not die but it lost its luster.

Progress sometimes comes from irritation. Distrust of Transylvania spurred religious groups to found their own colleges. The Presbyterians eventually succeeded in 1824 in gaining control of Centre College, originally

established by the state. The Roman Catholics established St. Joseph's College in 1819; the Methodists Cumberland College in 1822; and the Baptists Georgetown
College in 1829. The Kentucky frontier was not going
to be without schools to train the clergy of the varied
religions and to reproduce their respective orthodoxies.

Transylvania was the symbol of the classical culture
which made Lexington lay claim to the title of the
"Athens of the West," a title which many another town
on the advancing frontier would appropriate. This name
was a proud boast, and it sometimes indicated more
aspiration than achievement. Nevertheless, it showed
the hopes and dreams of that persistent group, "the
better element."

The Bluegrass section of Kentucky, of which Lexington was the cultural metropolis, rapidly changed
from a frontier to a sophisticated society. Southern
immigrants with enough money to buy slaves and extensive farm lands soon had established an agrarian
aristocracy not unlike Tidewater Virginia. An English
traveler in 1806 observed of Lexington that "a small
party of rich citizens are endeavoring to withdraw
themselves from the multitude. There are six or eight
families of these better sort who live in a handsome
manner, keep livery servants, and admit no person to
their table of vulgar manner or suspicious character." [17]
And it is perhaps significant that one of the most devas-
tating charges brought against Transylvania University
in 1825 by rabble-rousing Governor Desha was that it
was a "hotbed of aristocracy." [18] Politically Kentucky

prided itself on its fierce defense of democracy, but its democracy was a matter of definition depending on whether the citizen was a slaveholding planter in the Bluegrass or a rifleman in the clearings on the border of the Indian country.

The extent to which literate culture affected the general population in the new country cannot be accurately measured, but we know from surviving evidence that substantial numbers were interested in reading. Newspapers, magazines, and books soon found an important place in Kentucky life. Newspapers particularly flourished, for the region, cut off from the older centers in the East, had to supply its own media of communication.

John Bradford, a Virginian, published the first issue of the earliest newspaper, the *Kentucky Gazette*, in Lexington on August 11, 1787. Within a few years nearly every town in Kentucky could boast a newspaper. When Frankfort became the state capital, the revenue from legal printing made it a publication center. Papers sprang up overnight. Some lasted for only a few months but others proved hardy enough to survive financial strain or threats of bodily violence made against too outspoken editors. One newspaper, the *Western World*, established in Frankfort by John Wood and John Street, in 1806, had a crusading purpose which sounds uncannily like the present day, for its editors vowed to expose traitors and conspirators. They made capital of the Aaron Burr conspiracy but when they exposed a Spanish plot, one of the accused shot

Street.[19] Newspapers were violently partisan in the early days and the success of a paper often depended upon the capacity of an editor to fill his columns with colorful invective and to survive.

In addition to political discussion, advertisements, and a certain amount of news, chiefly culled from eastern publications, the newspapers supplied a variety of reading matter. They provided an outlet for hopeful authors who wanted to burst into verse or write an essay signed "Agricola" or some other classical pseudonym. They also printed useful information, practical advice, bits of verse reprinted from well-known authors, or essays, stories, and historical narratives—in short, anything which an editor believed would interest his readers. Furthermore, the newspaper printing offices published almanacs, broadsides, pamphlets, tracts, sermons, compilations of laws, and miscellaneous books—subject matter as varied as the range of human curiosity.[20]

To a frontier region where the establishment of legal processes must necessarily be one of the prime essentials in the creation of a civilized order, a knowledge of the laws of the new land and of legal procedures is highly important. For that reason it is no surprise that among the first books published were laws and related works. In 1792, the year that Kentucky became a state, John Bradford who had received an appointment as public printer brought out in Lexington the *Acts Passed at the First Session of the General Assembly* followed by various special laws and the proceedings of the legislature. Thereafter legal publications would multiply. In 1800 Bradford published *The General Instructor, or the Office, Duty, and Authority of Justices of the Peace, Sheriffs, Coroners and Constables in the State of Kentucky,* a work which must have been one of the most useful in a highly litigious country. Another book of similar purpose was Charles Humphreys' *A Constable's Guide Containing a Compilation of the Statutes of Virginia & Kentucky, and So Much of the Statutes & Common Law of England As Remains in Force in Kentucky Relating to the Office of Constable* (1813). Because of the impending war with England in 1811,[21] patriotism in Kentucky reached such a pitch that the legislature passed a law forbidding attorneys to cite precedents from English courts since July 4, 1776, but, directly or indirectly, the common law of England remained the basis of Kentucky jurisprudence. Between the years 1808 and 1819 William Littell brought out a five-volume edition of the *Statute Law of Kentucky.*

Next to laws, one of the great concerns of the settlers was a supply of school books. Most of them were imported from Philadelphia, but early local printers realized that profits could be made from the steady sale of elementary textbooks. John Bradford published in 1797 Samuel Wilson's *The Kentucky Grammar* and thereafter followed *The Kentucky Primer* (1798) and *The Kentucky Spelling-Book* (1798), published at Washington, Kentucky. Most famous of the textbooks was probably the *Kentucky Preceptor Containing a Number of Useful Lessons for Reading and Speaking* (1812) which is said to have been one of the books used by the youthful Abraham Lincoln. These titles did not mean a deviation from the conventional materials in older textbooks but represented merely an appeal to state pride.

Almost as important as textbooks were religious publications, some of which aroused intense controversial interest. For example, the Reverend Adam Rankin split the Presbyterian church in Kentucky wide open with a debate on psalmody. He heaped abuse on all who accepted Watts' hymns and versions of the Psalms, and made such a disturbance that the Transylvania Presbytery in 1792 tried him and declared his Lexington pulpit vacant. Thereupon he went over to the Associated Reformed Presbyterians and published *A Process in the Transilvania Presbytery* (1793) which gave his side of the argument over the use of Watts' *Psalms*. Rankin objected to Watts as giving too free a rendering and insisted that the church stick to a more literal translation. Rankin's tract was the precursor of many religious pamphlets and books, controversial, devotional and historical, which issued from the Kentucky presses. One significant pamphlet, widely reprinted, was a forecast of a bitter war of words ahead. It was the Reverend David Rice's *Slavery Inconsistent with Justice and Good Policy* (Lexington, 1792). The interest in Tom Paine's attack on orthodoxy was sufficient a few years later to prompt John Bradford to reprint a work of Bishop Richard Watson: *An Apology for the Bible, in a Series of Letters Addressed to Thomas Paine* (1797).

Kentucky printers found that historical and narrative

writings describing their region would find a ready market among the citizens of that proud and self-conscious region.[22] By 1812, a Frankfort printer felt justified in publishing Humphrey Marshall's *History of Kentucky,* which was expanded twelve years later into a two-volume work. More specialized works had already appeared. As early as 1799 John Bradford had brought out *An Account of the Remarkable Occurrences in the Life and Travels of Col. James Smith (Now a Citizen of Bourbon County, Kentucky) during His Captivity with the Indians.* William Littell published at Frankfort in 1806 *Transactions in and Concerning Kentucky from the First Settlement Thereof until It Became an Independent State in 1792.* Local histories like Dr. H. McMurtrie's *Sketches of Louisville and Its Environs* (Louisville, 1819) were eagerly read by a people conscious of their own importance.

But not all of the early literature published in Kentucky was prosaic. A somewhat unedifying citizen of Danville, known as Drunken Tom Johnson, was responsible for the first volume of native verses, the *Kentucky Miscellany,* published in Lexington in 1789. The quality of the poet may be seen in the epitaph which he wrote for himself:

> Underneath this marble tomb,
> In endless shades lies drunken Tom;
> Here safely moored, dead as a log,
> Who got his death by drinking grog.
> By whiskey grog he lost his breath
> Who would not die so sweet a death?[23]

The muse of poetry, however, would not confine her inspiration to one ribald verse maker. Kentucky newspapers echoed with the beat of heroic couplets as numerous contributors hastened to imitate Pope or James Thomson. *The Kentucky Gazette* for October 27, 1806 published an elevated piece from the pen of George Beck, poet, astronomer, artist, and director of an Academy for Young Ladies at Lexington. It was headed, "A New Translation of the Fifteenth Ode of Horace, or Prophecy of Nerceus, from which (according to Count Algorotti and Dr. Johnson) Gray took his beautiful Ode, *The Bard*." This was followed a month later by "Anacreon's Fifty-Fifth Ode." Imitations of Horace, some serious, some satirical, became a convention among the contributors to western papers. Verse writing was almost epidemic. So busy a lawyer as the versatile William Littell brought out in Louisville in 1814 *Festoons of Fancy, Consisting of Compositions Amatory, Sentimental, and Humorous*. The poet who attracted the most favorable comment from eastern critics was John M. Harney of Bardstown who in 1816 published anonymously in New York a long poem in heroic couplets entitled *Crystalina, a Fairy Tale*. It dealt with legends and superstitions of the Scottish Highlands. No work better illustrates the indebtedness of the Kentucky writer to tradition than Harney's *Crystalina*. Oblivious to the material around him, he had to go to the distant and unknown Scottish highlands for subject matter and to the correct English writers of the eighteenth century for models.

Stirred by a belletristic impulse more than one editor founded a literary magazine only to find that the country would not support an exclusively literary journal. The first enterprise of this sort started at Lexington with Daniel Bradford's *Medley, or Monthly Miscellany for the Year 1803, Containing Essays, on a Variety of Subjects, Sketches of Public Characters, Moral Tales, Poetry, &c.* Varied as was the fare promised, and moral as the tales might be, Bradford could not prolong the life of his journal beyond the year. Thereafter magazines sprang up from time to time, flourished briefly, and died. Something in the American atmosphere, especially the atmosphere of the South and West, is fatal to literary periodicals. They start with a glow of health and promise but soon perish. William G. Hunt's *Western Review,* first published at Lexington in 1819, lasted three years, but the country could not support it longer. The doctors at Transylvania University had somewhat better luck with the *Transylvania Journal of Medicine* which for a decade supplied scientific news. Finally the *Transylvanian,* a journal founded by a professor of mathematics at the University, combined scientific and literary articles and managed to persist in a precarious fashion.[24]

From the earliest years of settlement, general merchants carried books in their stocks. Along with dictionaries, grammars, rhetorics, spelling books, arithmetics, sermons, books of devotions, medical treatises and handbooks of surveying, John Duncan of Lexington advertised on Christmas Eve 1791 the works of Homer,

Xenophon, Virgil, Cicero, and Ovid, all probably in translation, and Ainsworth's *Latin Diction*. The advertisement of William Leavy on June 29, 1793 included Blackstone's *Commentaries, Pilgrim's Progress*, Chesterfield's *Letters*, Richardson's *Pamela*, Vattel's *Law of Nations*, and Tom Paine's *Works*. In the previous year, on December 8, 1792, James H. Stewart, bookseller and printer, advertised the opening of his store. Thomas Leishman, a bookbinder, announced in 1795 the moving of his shop. Apparently Lexington offered enough work to keep him busy. Booksellers in the Kentucky country were numerous enough to have some sort of organization by 1805, for on October 2 of that year the *Kentucky Gazette* chronicled a meeting at Lexington of the "Booksellers and Printers of the Western country" with John Bradford as president and T. Anderson as secretary.[25]

The first subscription library was organized on January 1, 1795 when a committee of citizens raised $500 to buy books in Philadelphia. A report in 1801 showed that the library had 750 volumes and in 1815 the Lexington library brought out a printed catalogue. Already the library of Transylvania University was famous throughout the country. It had begun with the gift of the private library of the Reverend John Todd of Louisa County, Virginia, and it had steadily grown.

Before the end of the eighteenth century Transylvania's library could boast many Greek and Roman authors (some of them in beautiful old editions), many of the key figures of seventeenth- and eighteenth-century thought, and a creditable collection of scientific works. One bill from Matthew Carey of Philadelphia in 1795 totaled £278 3s. 7d. and included the works of John Locke and Adam Smith. One little book, a sort of symbol of the transit of an older body of learning to the West, was presented to Transylvania in 1802 by James Moore, the first president. It is *Contra Octoginta Haereses* (Basle, 1544), in Greek. What makes it interesting is the fact that it had once belonged to William Cecil, Lord Burleigh.[26]

The diversity of books available and the scope of interest of potential readers are shown by a Lexington advertisement of John Mullanphy on September 11, 1798. He described "a choice and handsome collection of new books, just opened, consisting of many thousands of volumes of law, physic, divinity, history, novels, plays, German and French chap books, the whole to be sold at Philadelphia retail prices; also parcels of music for the violin, flute, etc., new songs, loaded horse whips, playing cards, men's shoes, fine and coarse. As I am returning to Baltimore this fall, I will give bargains either wholesale or retail. These goods to remain in town but two or three weeks." [27] Merchants did not haul thousands of books across the mountains from Philadelphia to Lexington on chance. They knew what would sell. In other towns in Kentucky, books were constantly advertised in the papers. Many of the works were of a practical nature—schoolbooks, lawbooks, and treatises on medicine, especially the ever-present volume of home remedies—but the public demand for novels, poetry, and other belles-lettres was keen.

The most popular authors, as one might surmise, were the standard writers in the English tradition. Shakespeare was the best known. The *Kentucky Gazette* for August 25, 1787 contained parodies on *Hamlet*, which may have been the first verse printed in Kentucky.[28] Editors and politicians quoted Shakespeare to make their points; schoolboys recited him; amateur actors performed the plays; booksellers nearly always advertised some version of his works; and professional dramatic companies could always depend upon Shakespeare to draw a crowd. Milton was early advertised in Kentucky newspapers and his works were occasionally imitated and more often quoted for their moral value. Alexander Pope was also exceedingly popular, at least for one work, *An Essay on Man*, which was reprinted in Lexington as early as 1804. Its epigrammatic couplets were constantly quoted and politicians gave themselves literary and moral stature by reciting its lines. *The Rape of the Lock* was also well-known. Indeed, Pope's satirical couplets found frequent imitators among would-be poets who contributed their own verse satires to the local papers. A little later, however, the romantic poets and novelists swept the Western frontier. Walter Scott, Byron, Southey, Thomas Moore, and Felicia Hemans were widely read. To whet the appetites of purchasers, newspapers announced forthcoming shipments of Scott and Byron.

There was very little "cultural lag" where these romantic writers were concerned. Editions of Scott and Byron reached Kentucky booksellers as soon after publication as transportation facilities could bring them. The vogue of these English authors was so great that even on more distant frontiers lonely men carried them in their luggage. For example, Osborne Russell, a trapper on the faraway Yellowstone wrote about a winter there in 1820: "We had some few books to read, such as Byron, Shakespeare, and Scott's works, the Bible, and Clark's *Commentary* on it, and other small works of geology, chemistry, and philosophy." [29]

The romanticism and sentimentality of early nineteenth-century English writers appealed to the frontier reader. He was too close to his own wild country to see the appeal of his forests, rivers, and savage Indians. That would come later when he would begin to interpret them through European eyes. But the wild country of Scotland, the land of the Crusaders, or Byron's romantic settings provided escape, entertainment, and constant fascination for Western readers.

As the Bluegrass country of Kentucky took on the outlines of settled life, it quickly fell into the pattern of the older civilization east of the mountains. A relaxed and pleasure-loving people, the well-to-do planters built comfortable and gracious houses, at first Georgian in inspiration and later classical under the influence of the Greek revival. Less well-to-do folk built simpler but neat brick houses. Cabinetmakers in

Lexington, Frankfort, and Louisville, working in native walnut and cherry woods, imitated English furniture fashionable at the time. Local silversmiths made cups for juleps and fashioned silverware of all sorts, as good as could be had from London.

The Kentucky towns quickly achieved the tone, the comforts, and the luxuries characteristic of urban society in the older regions. For example, Fortescue Cuming who traveled through Kentucky and Ohio in 1807-09 describes in *Sketches of a Tour to the Western Country* (Pittsburgh, 1810) the civilized appearance of Lexington and its approaches, the wide roads, the well-groomed fields and meadows, the spacious streets and houses "chiefly of brick, which since the year 1795 have rapidly taken the place of the original wooden ones, the comfortable inn, the luxuries to be had in the market, the variety of the manufactories, the seven fine distilleries," the handsome horses and carriages, and many other sights that pleased him. Especially worthy of note was a coffee house which would have been a credit to London. It had a "reading room for the benefit of subscribers and strangers in which are forty-two files of different newspapers, from various parts of the United States." [30] It also had tables for billiards, chess, and backgammon and everything to drink from native Bourbon to French wines.

Among Kentucky's principal sports, horse racing early came into its own with the establishing of a race track at Lexington in 1789. The traditions of the race-course went back to England via Virginia. The bluegrass pastures appeared to be especially endowed by the Creator to nourish fine horses, as the sour mash and charred oak kegs of the distillers appeared to have a special virtue which made Kentucky whisky particularly favored. Under these twin amenities, social life flourished, and all classes shared in their influence.

Kentuckians also began early to boast of the beauty of their women, and of their cultivation and charm. Numerous seminaries for young ladies undertook to instruct them in polite literature, French, drawing, painting, music, needlework, and dancing. Itinerant dancing masters were always welcome if they could stay reasonably sober. Some young ladies became sufficiently skilled in music to provide a market for pianofortes which were frequently advertised. Men took pride in their ability to play the violin or flute. A newcomer from Virginia in 1806 observed that "almost every young man of his acquaintance had a horse, a gun, and a violin," and "society seemed to be viewed as if it were intended for amusement alone." [31]

Music ranged from the self-conscious performance of cultivated young ladies on the pianoforte, to breakdowns played for country dances by a drunken fiddler. Immigrants had also brought with them the memory of traditional ballads sung for generations by their ancestors in England and Scotland, ballads which may still be heard in Kentucky mountain districts uncorrupted by radio and television. Religious groups enjoyed hymn singing and every bookseller stocked Watts' *Hymns*. Classes for improvement in hymn singing were held in schools and churches. Only the Associated Reformed Presbyterians looked with disfavor on music. They regarded even Watts' *Hymns* as profane and stuck austerely to literal versions of the Psalms.

Theatrical entertainment reached Kentucky before it had ceased to be frontier territory. Traveling wax-works which exhibited Washington at Valley Forge came to Lexington as early as 1797,[32] and strolling professional players made their way over the mountains in the wake of the pioneers. By the end of the eighteenth century Lexington had some sort of building known as a theatre where plays were given by amateur and perhaps by professional actors. During the first twenty years of the nineteenth century, both amateur and professional drama flourished in Lexington, Danville, Frankfort, and Louisville, which became the most important theatrical center in the state.[33] It enjoyed the advantage of being a river port accessible to traveling companies. Shakespeare was sure-fire entertainment; and the favorite plays of the professional companies were *Richard III, Othello, Hamlet, The Taming of the Shrew, The Merchant of Venice, Romeo and Juliet, Much Ado,* and *King Lear,* in that order.[34]

Kentucky's civilization, which developed so quickly in the fertile Bluegrass country, was not a precise duplicate of any region. Though the Virginia influence was strongest, it was not Virginia in little. Nor was it Pennsylvania, or Carolina, or New Jersey transferred to the other side of the mountains. It had absorbed all sorts of stocks and yet its agrarian society was predominantly influenced by the persistent British tradition. Kentuckians with jingoistic patriotism would have denied its great indebtedness to the country beyond the seas against which local politicians could always stir up a violent hatred. Had Kentuckians not been among the most ardent warmongers in 1811 and 1812? But in education, religion, literature, and learning, it looked back to Britain, sometimes without realizing it, for inspiration. The old tradition, sometimes filtered through the Atlantic seaboard civilization, sometimes coming direct through Scottish and English preachers and teachers and imported books, continued to shape the thinking of pioneers who rose above the cultural level of the Daniel Boone type.

Some influences were rejected, it is true, because of distasteful English connotations. The Episcopal Church, for instance, made small headway because it was associated with English tyranny.

Daniel Drake reported that he had never known any Episcopalians in his early days at Mayslick, Kentucky. "Indeed, I have no recollection of ever hearing the word pronounced," he added. "But I have heard much of the 'Church of England.' It was regarded merely as the persecuting ecclesiastical arm of the British government; an organized body of Arminians, enlisted in the service of despotism." [35] Yet evangelical Protestantism was of course just as British as Anglicanism. The Presbyterians who made such an impact on the Kentucky frontier were mostly of Scottish derivation, it is true, but they too were British and they insisted, as no other group, upon the maintenance of the classical heritage.

Though Kentuckians, influenced by isolation from the East, by the independence which their life on the frontier encouraged, and by the variety of their origins, developed a distinct personality, they drew upon the common credit of the American cultural inheritance, and the "better element" once more established outposts of learning and cultivation. Kentuckians would later carry their particular brand of civilization still farther to the West until it reached the Pacific Ocean.

THREE

Enlightenment in the Old West: North of the Ohio

A N observant architect once remarked that he
could take a day's drive across Ohio and
find architectural evidence suggesting every region of
the Atlantic seaboard from Maine to South Carolina.
These architectural vestiges indicate the diversity of
the origins of the people who settled Ohio in the early
nineteenth century. For the land north of the Ohio
River attracted an even greater variety of people than
the country to the south. The French had been the first
to realize the profits from trading posts on the rivers
feeding the Mississippi. After France lost Canada and
the Ohio Valley, a few Frenchmen lingered on in the
region but they were inundated by the tide of other
folk who swept into the country after the American
Revolution. They came in such swarms from New
England, for example, that Massachusetts and Connecticut took alarm lest their towns and villages should be
drained of population. From New York, New Jersey,
Pennsylvania, Virginia, Maryland, and the Carolinas
settlers made their way into the rich wooded land in
the Northwest Territory. Squatters in Kentucky heard
about the greater opportunities across the river and

emigrated. In origins, the immigrants into the North-west Territory were a mixed lot. The vast majority were of British stock, though there were a few Germans, Dutch, French, and Swiss. Of those of British background, the English and Scots predominated but there were some Welsh and Irish. The New England influence was strong, but not so strong as earlier historians made it appear. The culture of the Northwest Territory was not merely an extension of the steady habits of Connecticut or the Puritanism of Massachusetts Bay as some have believed. It was a medley of all with a much greater influence from the South than we have generally realized.

The most important staging area for the westward advance into Ohio and the Illinois country was Pittsburgh where the confluence of the Monongahela and the Allegheny rivers make the Ohio. Once a bone of contention between the French and the British, Pittsburgh was a crucial army post for many years, and by the end of the eighteenth century was already noted as a center of business and trade. By 1810, western Pennsylvania had a population of 210,000 and Pittsburgh, though it had a population of only 4,768, was the focal point of the region.[1] Fortescue Cuming who visited Pittsburgh in 1808 remarked that "as a trading or a manufacturing town, I think Pittsburgh for situation is not excelled in the United States and that it bids fair to become the emporium of the centre of the federal union."[2] Other visitors commented upon its industry and the diligence with which all of its citizens applied themselves to making money.

Nevertheless, Pittsburgh was something of a cultural center and helped to shape the civilization of the new regions farther to the West. The first newspaper west of the Alleghenies, the *Pittsburgh Gazette*, began publication in 1786 and became an important influence. Other papers and presses soon made publishing an important business in Pittsburgh. In 1800 Zadoc Cramer set up a bookbindery and presently opened a bookstore and printing press where he published almanacs and useful books. His *The Navigator Containing Directions for Navigating the Monongahela, Alleghany, Ohio, and Mississippi Rivers* had six editions between 1801 and 1808 and provided much information about the towns along the rivers. Cramer brought out religious works, travel narratives—including the first printed account of the Lewis and Clark expedition, the *Journal of Patrick Gass* (1807)—textbooks, miscellaneous literary pieces, and in 1813, a literary magazine called the *Western Gleaner* which was to be a "repository for arts, sciences, and literature." [3] Unhappily it quickly withered and died as did its predecessor the *Pioneer*, a journal in which the Reverend David Graham tried to imitate Addison. By 1816 more than one hundred titles had appeared from Pittsburgh presses. These included Pope's *Essay on Man*, a favorite with frontier readers, Goldsmith's *Vicar of Wakefield* and *Poetical Works*, and Allan Ramsay's *Gentle Shepherd*. [4]

Before the end of the eighteenth century at least one bookstore in Pittsburgh was selling the classics, law-books, history, philosophy, and belles-lettres. A circulating library was projected in 1788 by John Boyd but two weeks after his announcement in the *Gazette* he committed suicide,[5] a fate which has tempted more than one library promoter. Ten years later John Gilkison established a successful bookstore and circulating library. During the first fifteen years of the nineteenth century, bookstores and rental libraries flourished in Pittsburgh and in several other towns of western Pennsylvania. This outpost of civilization was clearly not barren of books. It even supported a small literary group of whom Hugh Henry Brackenridge was the most famous. At Pittsburgh in 1795, he published the third volume of *Modern Chivalry*, a picaresque romance inspired by *Don Quixote*.

The civilizing influence of the religious groups who dominated western Pennsylvania had an important effect on the culture of the region beyond. Most active were the Presbyterians. They were concerned about education and the transmission of classical learning. Although the Roman Catholics sent the first missionaries into western Pennsylvania and established schools there, they were overwhelmed in numbers by Protestants of whom the Presbyterians displayed the greatest zeal in ministering to the intellectual needs of the country. As early as 1802, the Presbyterian General Assembly created the Synod of Pittsburgh which thereafter took an active part in supplying ministers and

teachers to the frontier.[6] The Presbyterians were instrumental in establishing the first academies which
taught Greek, Latin, philosophy, history, literature, and
mathematics. One of the most vigorous exponents of
classical learning was the Reverend John McMillan,
a Princeton graduate, who came as a missionary to
western Pennsylvania, settled there in 1778, and later
founded Canonsburg Academy.

As in Kentucky the earliest schools in western Pennsylvania were the responsibility of the individual or of
religious groups. The state was slow about giving as-
sistance to frontier schools. Westerners however kept
up a constant agitation for state aid. They argued that
education was "favorable to liberty and that a free
government could not long persist without it."[7] In
1800 the legislature took some notice of the need for
academies by setting aside public land for their support. In 1802, it even incorporated a female seminary
at Meadville,[8] a recognition of the need for the education of women which would characterize later frontier
movements in education. By the time Fortescue Cuming
arrived in Pittsburgh in 1808, the town had clearly
made some educational progress, for he reported twelve
schoolmasters and four schoolmistresses who had set
up schools; but it must be admitted that this observer
like many who came after him was more impressed by
Pittsburgh's industries, including a "factory for making
clay smoking pipes,"[9] than by the cultural advantages.

Higher education for many years to come was principally in the hands of the Presbyterian clergy, and the

first two colleges founded in western Pennsylvania before 1815 were directed by them. Canonsburg Academy was translated into Jefferson College in 1802 under the supervision of the Reverend John Watson of Princeton. In 1806 Washington Academy changed its name to Washington College. "Its students were not long in importing from the East 'collegiate' customs—or costumes," observes the best cultural history of the region; "the boys wore as class uniforms flannel coats, green for the freshmen, blue for the sophomores, and red for the juniors; and the insignia for the seniors were top hats." [10] Surely the transmission of traditional culture could go no further! And half the graduates of Jefferson College before 1839 turned out to be ministers. The only institution in this section to show the influence of New England was Allegheny College, founded in 1815, whose first president was the Reverend Timothy Alden of Harvard.

The establishment of a civilized way of life in the British tradition at the gateway to the Northwest could not help influencing the quality of civilization beyond. Pittsburgh was more than an industrial town and entrepôt for goods to be distributed to the West. Though immigrants poured through Pittsburgh headed for the West, it never became a roaring city of sin like some of the staging areas in the later movements to the Far West. The stern Presbyterian control was too strong for that. Cuming remarked on the town's piety. "From the number of religious houses and sects, it may be presumed that the Sabbath is decently observed in

Pittsburgh," he commented, "and that really appears to be the case in a remarkable degree, considering it is so much of a manufacturing town, so recently become such, and inhabited by such a variety of people." [11] Settlers in the Ohio Valley and the country beyond did not necessarily have to look to the Atlantic seaboard for education, for teachers, for preachers, or even for books.[12] Western Pennsylvania had many of the elements of the civilization which they wanted to reproduce. In actuality, however, when they could, settlers in the new country tended to draw on the localities whence they had come for their cultural inspiration and nourishment.

The settlement of Ohio, Indiana, and Illinois resulted in an extraordinary conglomeration of groups from the Atlantic states. It would be too much to say that these settlers demonstrated at once the fusion of types, for they rarely fused. Their tendency at first was to huddle in distinctive separation. Fusion would come in time. But separate as the groups might be, they could not help affecting one another and the civilization which they developed.

The widest differences existed between the Southerners and the New Englanders. Southerners as a whole had an individualistic attitude in contrast to the community spirit characteristic of settlers from Massachusetts and Connecticut. New Englanders sometimes came as neighborhood units, sometimes under the leadership of a preacher or teacher just as they had moved out to found new towns in the seventeenth century. The New Englanders brought with them the reform spirit of the Puritans and a profound appreciation of education as a means of inculcating godliness. They were also shrewd and canny traders who quickly won a reputation for business acumen—and sometimes a name for sharp practice. The Southerners, who prided themselves on generosity, hospitality, and straightforward dealings, found little to praise in the New Englanders' preoccupation with shrewd mercantile acquisitiveness. A Kentucky newspaper in 1820 suggested that the people of the Western states ought to instruct their Congressmen to pass a law to prevent the importation of Yankees west of the Alleghenies.[13] The Yankees for their part despised what they considered the indolence, pride, arrogance, and violence of the Southerners. The Northerners exerted their genius in the perpetuation of orderly towns with schools, churches, and colleges as nearly like those of New England as they could achieve. The Southerners excelled in politics, oratory, and sometimes in journalism.

The political strength of the South in Ohio in the frontier period is usually forgotten. "The influx of people from Virginia, Pennsylvania, Kentucky, [and] Maryland was so early and so rapid that they took the political control out of the hands of federalistic New Englanders and brought Ohio into the union in 1802 as a Jeffersonian state," one commentator observes; "and a Jeffersonian state it remained for many years. The complexity of its population elements and their sectional distribution made Ohio a political microcosm of

the United States." [14] Indiana and Illinois likewise had
a large Southern immigration which affected both the
cultural and political quality of those states for many
years. Gradually New Englanders moved into Indiana
and Illinois and filtered down from the northern counties. The immigrants from the North found the Southerners in these states too shiftless to their liking. The
Southerners retorted that the Yankees were sly rogues
whose piety did not prevent their picking a neighbor's
pockets. Though the two groups were sometimes in
sharp conflict, they both made positive contributions to
the cultural complex of the region and inevitably influenced each other.

One of the most dramatic movements of New Englanders to the Northwest—and one reminiscent of the
seventeenth-century migrations—was inspired by that
extraordinary combination of preacher and promoter,
Manasseh Cutler, and a Revolutionary general, Rufus
Putnam. Cutler was a Yale graduate and a Congregational preacher, but more than that, he was a master
land speculator and lobbyist. On October 27, 1787, he
signed a contract with the Treasury Board in behalf
of the Ohio Company of Associates for a million and a
half acres of land at the confluence of the Muskingum
and Ohio rivers. For this tract he paid eight cents an
acre. It would be pleasant if we could describe the
New Englanders' migration to the Ohio tract under
the personal leadership of Parson Cutler as Thomas
Hooker had led his followers to the Connecticut Valley. Actually General Putnam led the trek, the last

portion of which was by boat, and Parson Cutler drove out later in a sulky. In deference to New England tradition, Putnam named one of the flatboats which floated his party of 60 down the Ohio the "Mayflower." The settlers arrived at their destination on April 7, 1788, and began building a village which they presently named Marietta, curiously enough, after Queen Marie Antoinette of France.

Marietta was typically New England in quality, and most of its early citizens had Puritan names long known in Massachusetts, Connecticut, New Hampshire, and Rhode Island. Unlike the seventeenth-century Puritans, however, these settlers were not willing to be ruled by the clergy. Eager as they were to establish churches and schools, many of them had imbibed Jeffersonian principles and were determined that church and state should be forever separate.[15] Nevertheless, the contract of the Ohio Company provided that one section of land in each township should be set aside to support public education and another to maintain religion. This was in keeping with the previous land ordinances. The Ordinance of 1785 had prescribed that each township should be laid out with thirty-six numbered sections of 640 acres each, and that Section 16 should be reserved for public education. The Ordinance of 1787 had declared that "religion, morality, and knowledge, being necessary to good government and the happiness of mankind, schools and the means of education shall forever be encouraged." In keeping with the spirit of these ordinances and their own inherited doctrines,

Cutler, Putnam, and their associates set aside Section 16 for schools and Section 29 for religion.[16]

Cutler also persuaded Congress to add to his purchase two additional townships which might be used for the support of a university. This precedent later proved beneficial to higher education in other areas of the West where it was adopted as a pattern in subsequent allocations of public land. The revenue from the land allocated to religion was to be divided among the recognized sects, and this, of course, became a fruitful source of controversy and rancor. In a short time Marietta was a neat and orderly town with classical names for its main subdivisions. Putnam called the fortified stockade Campus Martius and set up a school inside. A few years later Cuming remarked that "Marietta is principally inhabited by New Englanders, which accounts for the neat and handsome style of building displayed in it," [17] and a New England visitor commented on the neatness and thrift of the citizens of Marietta and its environs in contrast to the neglect on the south side of the Ohio which depended upon slave labor.[18] In the first year of settlement an enthusiastic citizen wrote back to describe the progress: "Our first ball was opened about the middle of December, at which were fifteen ladies, as well accomplished in the manners of polite circles as I have ever seen in the old States. I mention this to show the progress of society in this new world where I believe we shall vie with, if not excel, the old States in every accomplishment necessary to render life agreeable and happy." [19]

When Marietta celebrated its centenary in 1888, President Rutherford B. Hayes with the patriotic fervor of a politician declared that "Putnam and his followers were the best educated men the world ever knew. For eight years, from 1775 to 1783, they went to school to George Washington." [20]

For some time Marietta remained the only pure New England settlement, but as such, it served as a beacon and an example because of its encouragement of religion, education, and "intellectual improvement." No roistering wild west town was this. It was almost as sober as New Haven or Dedham.

The next town to develop in Ohio—Cincinnati—also became a cultural center which in variety and influence quickly outstripped Marietta. In 1788 a New Jersey land speculator, John Cleves Symmes, purchased something like a million acres along the Ohio River and stretching north between the Miami and Little Miami rivers. Immediately Symmes began to advertise the advantages of this tract, known as the Miami or Symmes Purchase, and in the late autumn and early winter, immigrants began to trickle into the new country. Most of the early settlers came from New Jersey but soon Kentuckians were moving across the river in response to tales of rich lands farther on, and within a few years immigrants were swarming into the territory from all sections. The first important settlement was called learnedly, Losantiville, meaning the "town opposite the Licking River" but in 1790 General Arthur St. Clair, the territorial governor, changed it to Cincinnati in honor of the society of Revolutionary officers of which he was a member. The town became the chief trading center of the rich back country. According to Daniel Drake, who had published there in 1815 his . . . *View or Picture of Cincinnati,* the Symmes Purchase had 15,000 inhabitants by 1800; ten years later, Hamilton County alone, of which Cincinnati was the county seat, had more than 15,000. In 1810 the town had a population of 2,320 and two years later, 4,000. In 1815 Drake estimated the population of Cincinnati at 6,000. Cincinnati was rapidly overtaking Pittsburgh in population and was becoming almost as important as a trading town.[21]

Like Manasseh Cutler, Symmes had provided for education and religion by allocating Sections 16 and 29 in each township for their support. The promise to maintain religion and learning was one of the attractions emphasized in his publicity. So well did Cincinnati succeed that in 1815 it had three Protestant churches—Presbyterian, Baptist, and Methodist—a Quaker Meeting House, three banks, three newspapers, a steam mill, a university, and a library.[22] This symmetry of institutions—cultural, financial, and industrial—would form a pattern which towns throughout the expanding nation would try to emulate. But Drake, the town's chronicler, was not altogether satisfied. Although Cincinnati had ample resources for the "rectification of spirits and the distillations of cordials," he pointed out that except for sign painting and engraving, "in the fine arts we have not anything to boast." [23] Something seemed a little out of balance. Lexington had already appropriated the name of "Athens of the West," but Cincinnati was ambitious and full of civic pride. The town would presently announce that she was "Queen City of the West." If she could not immediately outstrip Lexington in classical culture, she would claim a crown for general improvement and amplitude of opportunity. Actually Cincinnati rapidly became the most important town in the West for publishing and book distribution; it provided the most varied educational opportunities; and it acquired a remarkable group of cultivated citizens and civic leaders.

Though Cincinnati was compounded of people from many sources, such was the unifying effect of the traditional cultural patterns of the East that it developed a certain homogeneity by assimilating influences from Virginia, the Carolinas, Pennsylvania, and New England. "There is no state in the Union which has not enriched our town with some of its more enterprising or restless citizens," Drake remarked: "nor a kingdom of the west of Europe whose adventurous or desperate exiles are not commingled with us. To Kentucky, and the states north of Virginia—to England, Ireland, Germany, Scotland, France, and Holland, we are most indebted." [24] Although Drake was too close to see how completely the conventional cultural pattern, inherited ultimately from Great Britain, would shape the new civilization, he added a few observations on the qualities common to the population as a whole: "Those which at present can be perceived are industry, tem-

perance, morality, and love of gain. With a population
governed by such habits and principles, the town must
necessarily advance in improvements at a rapid rate.
This, in turn, excites emulation and precludes the idle-
ness which generates prodigality and vice. Wealth is
moreover pretty equally distributed, and the prohibi-
tion of slavery diffuses labor." [25]

The growth of Cincinnati might be taken as a symbol
of the development characteristic of the American city
of the West. However small and unpromising, Western
frontier towns made large claims for the future. Each
thought it would become, not only the biggest, but
the best. Unhappily we have too often equated size
and goodness. Nevertheless, even those towns most
blatantly commercial, or those in which the raucous
and the lawless temporarily took possession, had a
saving remnant who tenaciously clung to an ideal of
civic improvement. They were determined to establish
churches, schools, and libraries, to make their town as
civilized as any city on the Eastern seaboard. Often
their efforts were pathetic, but the dream was there,
and the dream was important. Usually in the end, the
tenacious, civic-minded folk won. Perhaps the most
significant fact in the urban development of the United
States in the nineteenth century was the determination
—and the success—of the "better element" in reproducing the essentials of what they believed necessary to a
civilized life.

Marietta and Cincinnati were the prototypes of scores
of towns which developed in the Northwest Territory

during the frontier period. Some like Marietta were characteristically New England in type. Others like Cincinnati reflected diversity of population and illustrated a new nationalizing tendency, an assimilation of divergent groups. Each type reacted upon the others. The New Englanders, possessed of crusading zeal and the Puritan notion that they were the elect of God, exerted more influence in some areas than their numerical strength would indicate. Small enclaves of New Englanders penetrated the whole area, but New England's greatest strength lay in the north, especially in the Western Reserve along Lake Erie where Connecticut sent her citizens to populate the western lands which that state had shrewdly reserved from the general cession to the Federal government. Southern enclaves, likewise, pushed inland from across the Ohio. Chillicothe, the first capital of Ohio, was essentially a Southern town; Columbus, the later capital, was first settled principally by Southern and Middle State people; and Dayton had a Southern increment that persisted until the Civil War and resulted in violent riots at that time.

Someone has observed that if a town built a Congregational Church and a college, it was certainly of New England origin. If it boasted a Presbyterian Church and a distillery, it had been settled by Kentuckians or Virginians. All of these influences were important. But one should hasten to add for the benefit of the literal-minded that New Englanders had no monopoly of education nor were Southerners the only consumers and manufacturers of spirits.

Religion was a powerful factor in the civilization of the Northwest Territory, as indeed, it had been on all previous frontiers, but the new country had a greater variety of religions than had flourished in any other territory. Into the Northwest streamed not only most of the older denominations but many new sects and cults.

The great revival known as the Second Awakening which moved from New England to the West at the turn of the century had tremendous repercussions, first in Kentucky, and then in Ohio, Indiana, and Illinois. It was confined to no single denomination. Methodists, Baptists, Presbyterians, and Congregationalists alike shared in its frenzy, which left sinners jerking, frothing, and moaning in fear of damnation. It came as an aftermath of a religious slump which followed the Revolution. For a time many literate folk had loudly praised Tom Paine's *Age of Reason*, quoted Voltaire and the French skeptics, and were open in their infidelity. On a lower level, there was drunkenness, gambling, debauchery, and scandalous excesses of all kinds. Christian folk expressed fear that the depravity, which seemed even greater on the untrammeled frontier, would destroy all standards of morality in the hinterland. But the revivalists who swarmed into the backcountry put an end to complacence about iniquity. Some sympathetic observers of the revival movement commented that even profane teamsters and boatmen had modified their language and that rowdies in the river ports no longer spent their leisure hours in drinking and gouging out the eyes of their fellows. The hysteria of the revival has been greatly emphasized. Its excesses have given the impression of a complete orgy of religious emotion. Yet one of the leading church historians in this country thinks that on the frontier the net effect was beneficial.[26] One unexpected influence, however, was the impetus it gave to schisms and divisive movements, especially among the Baptists and Presbyterians.

Although the Roman Catholics were the first Christians in the Northwest, and they remained there and gained ground slowly, the most active and successful missionaries in the post-Revolutionary period of settlement were the Presbyterians. By a Plan of Union adopted in 1801 by Presbyterians and Congregationalists, settlers of these faiths in a new community could combine to establish a church. In practice the Presbyterians benefited most from the scheme, and in Ohio and Illinois, many churches which started out Congregationalist, ended up Presbyterian.[27] Presbyterians of Scottish background were a determined folk. It was one of their number who prayed, "Oh Lord, grant that I may always be right, for Thou knowest that I am hard to turn."

Though the Presbyterians and Congregationalists were outnumbered by Methodists and Baptists, they made the greater contribution to the cultural uplift of the country, for they insisted rigidly upon an educated ministry and they implied that education provided a path to salvation. The Baptists at first took a contrary view. Their preachers were frequently farmers on week days and unpaid—and untrained—preachers on Sunday. The Methodists occupied a sort of middle ground. They did not insist upon a professionally trained ministry, but their requirements were somewhat higher than the Baptists, and they had a central organization that exercised supervision of the itinerant circuit riders. Actually, these hard-riding, fearless Methodist preachers who rode the endless frontier circuits performed a far greater service in civilizing the people than we have recognized. They carried tracts which they often taught people to read. They insisted upon Bible reading as a mark of Christian piety. And a little later in the frontier period, they preached in behalf of public education. Of all the Protestant faiths, the Episcopalians were the least adapted to frontier conditions and made the least impression upon the Northwest.

Coincidental with the flourishing of recognized sects in the Northwest were several cults which found there a refuge, if not always cordial hospitality. The Shakers, English in origin, sent missionaries to Kentucky, Ohio, and Indiana after the Second Awakening and managed to establish several communities. They looked upon marriage, along with learning, as the source of human iniquity and both men and women took vows of celibacy.[28] Naturally so unorthodox a doctrine solidified the older religions against them. Also a celibate cult were the followers of the German, George Rapp, who in 1814 founded a communal settlement at New Harmony on the Wabash in Indiana. They proved highly successful farmers but sold out in 1824 to a Utopian social cultist, Robert Owens, and moved to a site on the Ohio below Pittsburgh, which they called Economy. The Mormons also had a brief period in Ohio, from 1831, when they came to Kirtland, until 1840 when they moved to Nauvoo, Illinois. Unlike the Shakers and the Rappites, they glorified marriage, but when Joseph Smith in 1843 received a revelation commending polygamy, they became even more unpopular. But theirs is a story of the later West.

Whatever the nature of frontier religion, it had an increasing importance to the settlers of the Northwest Territory as they gradually shaped themselves into farming communities, villages, and towns. Churches dotted the landscapes and exercised a profound influence not only in spiritual comfort but as a means of providing social cohesion to their congregations, if not always to the community as a whole. With the exception of small pockets of Roman Catholics, the German Reformed Church, German Lutherans, and a few minor sects and cults, the prevailing religions were the Protestant dissenting faiths which despite schisms and controversies had undergone little essential change since they originated in England and Scotland. Not until long after the frontier period would the British Protestant tradition have a serious challenge in this region. That fact is of tremendous importance in assessing the quality of the country's citizenry and the influence that they exerted as they moved across the country. For the Northwest Territory provided an enormous reservoir of emigrants who continually pushed farther West until they at last reached the Pacific.

Closely related to religion was education. Even though many of the new tracts in the Northwest provided public land for the support of education, actually for many years such support was inadequate, and education remained the concern of the individual or of religious groups. The most ardent in the advocacy of education were the Presbyterians and Congregationalists, those hard-headed founders of schools and colleges which in time dotted Ohio as no other region.

Numerous as schools and colleges were to become later, actually in the early period this frontier showed less educational progress than Kentucky and Pennsylvania. Despite the provision of land for the support of education the notion that every child was entitled to a free education at the state's expense would have been regarded as an absurdity. The consumers were expected to pay for education. The public land merely helped to provide facilities where a parent might pay to send his child to school. Missionaries, preachers, and charitable teachers sometimes gave lessons to the children of the poor for little or nothing, but there was no systematic method of insuring even their elementary education.[29] Nevertheless the struggle of the pioneers to make it possible for their children to acquire the elements of traditional learning ought to be instructive for our generation, accustomed as we are to accept free education as we do the air we breathe.

Scotch Presbyterian ministers and teachers who came from Virginia, Kentucky, and Pennsylvania were the first to lay a foundation for education in the Northwest. They were followed by Congregationalist teachers and preachers from New England. In addition, "keeping a school" became the occupation of practically anybody who needed to supplement his subsistence. Struggling lawyers and doctors sometimes taught school on the side. Itinerant schoolmasters, occasionally much addicted to the bottle, if we may believe contemporary letters and diaries, found it profitable to set up as teachers before they moved on to fresher fields. Where settlers lived in compact groups schools flourished. The isolated pioneer, however, could only hope to pass on such book learning as he knew, or to benefit from such instruction as a passing circuit rider might give the children.

If the struggle for existence kept most frontier citizens from thinking much about education, American communities have nearly always developed a few strong-minded souls who made educational development their particular province. Such a man was Daniel Drake of Cincinnati. Throughout his life he busied himself with projects for schools and colleges. To him is due the eminence for a time of Cincinnati's medical schools and for the stimulation of scientific interest in Ohio. He also labored to perpetuate the liberal arts and to provide for elementary schools. Other communities had similar sponsors of education.

As early as 1790, Rufus Putnam wrote back to Manasseh Cutler from the new town of Marietta expressing his hope that classical learning might soon be established there: "There are several academies in the neighboring parts of Pennsylvania, Virginia, and Kentucky, where the Latin and Greek are taught, and Muskingum Academy at Marietta is at present, and I trust, will always in the future be supplied with a master capable of teaching the languages, and I think it cannot be long before Latin schools are established in several other places in the territory." [30] Putnam was no polished classicist, but to him Latin and Greek symbolized a link with the ancient tradition of learning which he hoped would have a beneficent influence upon culture—and the price of land—in the Ohio Purchase.

The educational theories of Joseph Lancaster, an English Quaker, attracted the attention of several Ohio communities. Lancaster devised a scheme for the supervision of the younger pupils by the older—an ideal arrangement where teachers were scarce and schools overcrowded. His schools also emphasized an elaborate system of rewards and punishments. Cincinnati, Dayton, and other towns established Lancastrian schools between 1812 and 1818. The Cincinnati Lancaster Seminary, originally an outgrowth of separate projects by Methodists and Presbyterians, in 1819 developed into Cincinnati College, which for a short time rivaled

Transylvania. But like most of the Middle Western colleges, its progress was hindered by intramural quarrels. Finally in 1835 it acquired as president, William H. McGuffey, a Presbyterian preacher, whose pious and patriotic textbooks influenced generations of school children.

Cincinnati was more solicitous than most other towns for the education of women, and several "female academies" flourished there before the end of the third decade of the nineteenth century. The *Western Monthly Review* for April 1830 boasted that eleven gold medals had been awarded at commencement to graduates of Cincinnati Female College for skill in Latin, Greek, French, mathematics, music, and painting.[31] The beginnings of the West's concern for the education of women on an equal footing with men can be discerned in the early development of female academies and colleges in the Northwest Territory.

Manasseh Cutler the promoter dreamed of a university grandiose enough to match the territory which he wanted to advertise north of the Ohio. He proposed an institution to be named American Western University and the town in the woods where it would grow he christened Athens. In 1804 the legislature of the new state of Ohio chartered the college as Ohio University. The first head of the school, Jacob Lindly, was a Presbyterian minister and a graduate of Princeton and for many years the Presbyterians dominated the college. In 1839 McGuffey was translated from Cincinnati to Athens to be president.

Cincinnati tried to obtain the university established on the college township lands in the Miami Purchase, but after a political tug-of-war, the legislature ordered a town laid out in the woods and named it Oxford. There in 1809 Miami University was founded—on paper. Not until 1824 when Robert Hamilton Bishop, an enlightened Scot, became president, did it develop into an institution of higher learning. From his eminence in Cincinnati, Drake remarked sourly in 1815 "that it will attain to the rank of a second rate college in the course of the present century, where it is now fixed, no well informed person has the courage to predict." [32] But Drake reckoned without Bishop, who had taught at Transylvania. Despite faculty bickering and political interference Bishop made Miami a powerful influence in the region. His curriculum emphasized both the Bible and the classics, good morality, good manners, and good literature. Yet he did not neglect science, mathematics, and such useful subjects as surveying. In 1829 Bishop advertised a "Farmer's College" but he did not mean courses in agriculture. It was merely the regular curriculum tailored to three years to suit busy farmer boys. "Literary and scientific knowledge is no longer to be the exclusive property of a few professional men," he declared. "It is to become the common property of the mass of the human family. . . . It is of vast importance . . . that a reasonable proportion of the farming interest should be qualified to move on at the head of all improvements in their immediate neighborhood." [33] Education for leadership by providing the solid substance of traditional learning was his ideal. What Yale, Dartmouth, and Princeton were to the East, Miami should be to the country north and west of the Ohio River.

Highbrow critics, especially if they were from England or New England, could find little good to say about the cultural level of Indiana in the frontier days. Yet even Indiana Territory, as early as 1804, was hopeful of higher learning. Congress in that year set aside a township to support a seminary, and the territorial legislature passed a resolution declaring that "for as much as literature, and philosophy, furnish the most useful and pleasing occupations, improving and varying the enjoyments of prosperity, affording relief under the pressure of misfortune, and hope and consolation in the hours of death," [34] it would authorize the establishment of Vincennes University. The legislature, like many later law-making bodies in the West, wanted to specify the courses to be taught, but it is interesting that it did not require "practical" courses. A seminary of learning was not for such purposes. The legislature decided that Vincennes University should teach "the Latin, Greek, French, and English languages, mathematics, natural philosophy, logic, rhetoric, and the law of nature and of nations." [35] As might be expected, the Presbyterians gained control, as they did over the seminary chartered at Bloomington in 1820 which later grew into Indiana University.

Opposition to the dominance of education by the Presbyterians was growing in various regions, but in

Indiana it came to a head in an act of the legislature in 1828 changing Bloomington Seminary into Indiana College. That act specified that no sectarian beliefs should be taught, and it also made a significant modification of the curriculum requirements by providing for the education of youth in the "American" language.[36] The frontier was becoming self-consciously "American" and the Middle West was beginning to develop certain traits which would grow into isolationism.

An amazing proliferation of colleges occurred in the Northwest from about 1825 onward. Their growth was partly a result of civic pride and local promotion and partly a result of missionary enterprise. Towns competed for the establishment of seminaries and colleges even if they later failed to support them. The eagerness for colleges is indicative of the premium which the new country, often naively, placed on higher learning.[37] A college brought prestige to a town, increased property values, and improved morality—or so it was believed. The activity of the Home Missionary Society, organized in 1826 on a national scale by Congregationalists and Presbyterians, also stimulated the founding of colleges. Even the Baptists, who at first had scorned learning, came to realize that a supply of competent preachers depended on regional colleges. Most of the sects hastened to found colleges. At length the Episcopalians, who had exerted a very small influence as yet in the West, raised money in England and in 1824 received a charter for Kenyon College.

To the zeal of the American Home Missionary Society and similar groups the frontier region owed many civilizing influences. Though Congregationalists had taken the initiative in the organization of this Society they at first advised missionaries going into the West to accept Presbyterian ordination. Eventually men from Congregational colleges, notably Yale, assumed direction of the Society and became diligent propagators of Congregational schools. A group of young men at Yale in 1828, nominally Presbyterian but Congregational in doctrine, formed themselves into a band and vowed to devote themselves to the salvation of Illinois. This "Yale Band" was responsible in the following year for the founding of Illinois College at Jacksonville. From this time onward Yale began to overtake Princeton as an educational influence on the Western frontier. The Yale men's educational ideals, however, were not very different. If anything Yale men tended to be a little stricter and more moralistic even than Presbyterians from Princeton. Both however placed great emphasis on classical learning as a way to teach sound morality. Some of the denominational colleges, Wabash, for example, combined manual labor with learning in order to keep the students fit and reduce the cost of education. The thrifty men who organized these colleges thought physical education ought to pay its way. Football was yet undreamed of, and splitting rails was regarded as conducive to high thinking as well as plain living.

The most crusading of the colleges was Oberlin, which combined Whig politics with piety. It was established in the Western Reserve district of Ohio in

1833 by John Shipherd and Philo Stewart, followers of Charles G. Finney, an evangelical Presbyterian who had rebelled against the strict Calvinism of the orthodox wing of the church. Oberlin opened its doors to two oppressed groups, Negroes and women, and at once became the target of hostile critics. Anti-abolitionists damned it for carrying on a meddling propaganda, and anti-feminists accused it of encouraging promiscuity and undermining the institution of marriage. Actually it was dismally strait-laced. One of the first books bought for its library was *Dyspepsy Forestalled & Resisted* (1830) by Edward Hitchcock of Amherst College, a treatise on health, which advocated abstemiousness, exercise, fresh air, and bathing—even in winter. The founders of Oberlin also came under the influence of Dr. Sylvester Graham and William A. Alcott, who equated godliness and physical culture. Whereupon they adopted rules advocated by these worthies and decreed that Oberlin should do its thinking on a vegetarian diet. The college banned tea, coffee, meat, fish, pepper and other condiments, gravy, butter, and practically anything with taste enough to be a temptation of the flesh. Any alcoholic beverage was described as the devil's poison, and the smoke from tobacco as the fumes of hell. Its curriculum emphasized religious instruction but it included standard courses in the classics, philosophy, mathematics, natural philosophy, and history. Despite a barrage of criticism, Oberlin flourished and in time sent out missionaries to found other colleges, if not precisely in its own image, at least akin to it in moral purposefulness and ascetic fear of frivolity.[38] Oberlin was the spiritual parent of reform movements and pious colleges from Ohio to California.

The aim of the denominational colleges, for the most part evangelical Protestant in doctrine, was moral improvement, but it was something more than that. They believed that good morality was dependent upon the cultivation of the mind, upon knowledge derived from the traditional reservoirs. Though many of these colleges were institutions of higher learning only in name and were often the objects of ridicule from English travelers, they performed an important function in bringing a modicum of classical education to a raw and ill-equipped country. A young graduate of Bowdoin and a teacher of the classics in Louisville, Edmund Flagg, took a trip through Illinois in 1836 and was impressed, among other things, with the colleges he saw. They were the hope of the country, he believed, the conservators of old learning and the teachers of good manners and morals. "What reflecting mind does not hail with joy these temples of science elevating themselves upon every green hill and broad plain of the West, side by side with the sanctuaries of our holy religion!" Flagg exclaims. "It is *baptized intelligence,* which alone can save this beautiful valley, if indeed it is to be saved from the inroads of arbitrary rule and false religion; which is to hand down to another generation our civil and religious immunities unimpaired." [39] These colleges bequeathed a doctrine and ideal to later generations. Evangelical denominations to this day believe that they have a special mission to maintain colleges as a bulwark of what they describe as Christian education.

The propagation of literacy and literary culture is never the exclusive privilege of official agencies like schools and colleges. Indeed, unofficial and even disapproved agencies are sometimes more effective. Local newspapers and magazines, books picked up in the general stores, the performance of plays, political oratory, even court trials, all helped to educate the rank and file of the population on the frontier.

No previous frontier ever had so many newspapers as burst upon the populace of the Northwest Territory. The most recent historian of the region comments of the newspapers that they provided "a literature so voluminous and rich in content that it would be impossible for any one man or group of men to digest and exhaust it." [40] And he quotes a sarcastic passage from Mrs. Trollope which is worth repeating: "In truth, there are many reasons which render a very general diffusion of literature impossible in America. I can scarcely class the universal reading of newspapers as an exception to this remark; if I could, my statement would be exactly the reverse, and I should say that America beat the world in letters." Americans, especially those she met in Cincinnati, were too busy to read anything except newspapers, Mrs. Trollope believed. "It is for this reason, I presume," she added, "that every *American newspaper* is more or less a magazine, wherein the merchant may scan while he holds out his hand for an invoice,

'Stanzas by Mrs. Hemans,' or a garbled extract from Moore's *Life of Byron*." [41] In trying to account for the mediocrity of American literature Mrs. Trollope a little later remarked that "the immense exhalation of periodical trash, which penetrates into every cot and corner of the country, and which is greedily sucked in by all ranks, is unquestionably one great cause of its inferiority. Where newspapers are the principal vehicles of the wit and wisdom of a people, the higher graces of composition can hardly be looked for." [42]

Whatever may be the truth of Mrs. Trollope's contentions about the baleful influence of the periodical press on great literature, there is no question about her testimony concerning the popularity of newspapers and magazines. That has been a characteristic of Americans from that day to this. Periodicals still furnish most of our literary fare. They were even more important on the frontier where other forms of reading matter were relatively scarcer.

Frontier periodicals not only supplied an enormous amount of entertainment and information but they also provided an outlet for the publication of the works of incipient authors. Backwoods poets, imitating Horace, Pope, or Scott according to their taste, could publish their efforts in the papers. The local poetry of the day ran to lachrymose sentimentality or broad satire. Editors occasionally exercised some discrimination but most published anything that would not land them in court for libel. Two of the early papers, *Liberty Hall* at Cincinnati and the *Western Spectator* at Marietta achieved a degree of literary merit, probably reflecting the quality of their respective communities. The editor of *Liberty Hall,* a Congregational preacher named John W. Browne, appealed to his subscribers to submit articles on "agriculture and commerce, the biographical memoirs of persons notable for their patriotism, philosophy, poetry, science, and piety," and especially "moral and instructive essays." [43]

Few towns of any size in the Northwest Territory lacked a weekly newspaper. The establishment of a paper was usually one of the first enterprises to get under way. Most of them were violently partisan in politics and periods of political furor always produced a few new papers to support the rival candidates. Editors exhausted their vocabularies of invective and encomium and from the depths of their literary knowledge they drew quotations to describe the objects of their editorials.

In contents, political news took first place in the Western papers, with a miscellany of domestic and foreign despatches clipped from the freshest Eastern papers that came to hand. Local news varied in accordance with the editor's opinion of its importance. If everybody in the community already knew about a local event by the time he went to press, it might receive very scant treatment. Always there was room for contributed articles of almost any kind, and always the editor had on hand "fillers" which he might run when there was a dearth of anything else. Frequently Western papers reprinted pieces from popular British authors—Burns,

Pope, Byron, and Scott were favorites. The editor of
the *Indiana Gazette* was so hard up for copy in August
1804 that he reprinted excerpts from Oliver Goldsmith's *Essays*.[44] The quantity of British literature
reproduced in this fashion was considerable, and its
effect was not lost upon frontier readers.

Westerners were themselves conscious that periodicals were important in the development of their society.
Many of the editors were highly literate men, though
they had often obtained their schooling as apprentices
to a printer. Benjamin Franklin, they were fond of
reminding themselves, got his education, not in clois-
tered halls, but in front of a type case. An Indiana editor, John W. Dillon, expressed the Westerner's concept
of the value of newspapers in reproducing traditional
civilization, "The newspaper is the great instrument of
civilization," he wrote in 1836. "All the books ever
written are but a feather in the scale compared with
newspapers as a means of affecting the mass. . . . It is
almost entirely to the influence of newspapers that the
superior intelligence of the middle classes is to be attributed." [45] And it was a middle-class civilization that
we were building, buttressed by ideas, habits of thought,
and behavior chiefly inherited from the middle-class
civilization of Great Britain.

More deliberate efforts to encourage a literary culture were made by the editors of magazines which
sprang up in the Northwest as they had in Kentucky.
Though the mortality of literary magazines in America
is the highest of any form of periodical publication,

editors never lose hope. Little magazines on the frontier bloomed for a day, faded, and died. As early
as 1819, Cincinnati had a belletristic periodical, the
Literary Cadet which was soon absorbed by the *Western Spy* and continued until 1823 as the *Western Spy
and Literary Cadet*. It was succeeded by the *Cincinnati
Literary Gazette* which lasted a year. For the next forty
years Cincinnati had a succession of literary, religious,
and scientific journals, including a number devoted
exclusively to the interests of women.[46] But the soil of
Cincinnati was no more favorable than that of Lexington or any other Western community. Timothy Flint,
preacher, novelist, and historian, established in Cincinnati in 1827 *The Western Magazine and Review,*
soon changed to *The Western Monthly Review,* which
lasted three years. Flint announced that "mere ordinary
or commonplace writing shall find no admittance to our
pages" but he soon discovered that poetry "of domestic
fabric" and "tales, moral essays, and articles of natural
history" which he sought were almost as elusive as
paid-up subscribers. His periodical was followed by
The Illinois Monthly Magazine established at Vandalia
in 1830 by James Hall, another versatile man of letters,
who had even less success than Flint. After two years
he gave up and moved to Cincinnati because of the
literary activity in that metropolis. The mere naming
of all the literary periodicals would exceed the scope of
the present discussion. Fleeting as they were, they indicate the persistent zeal of an energetic and optimistic
group of men and women of literary taste.

From the earliest period, books occupied a larger place in the interests of frontiersmen than we would suppose. The general stores carried a surprising variety of books. The newspapers advertised long lists of books "just arrived," and often served as bookstores. Occasionally book auctions were held. From the beginning Cincinnati and Marietta were important sources of books, but other towns, notably Chillicothe and a little later Vincennes, were sources of supply for their areas. For the most part the books were standard works of English literature. Eighteenth-century writers like Addison and Steele, Pope, James Thomson, Goldsmith, Dr. Johnson, and Edward Young were common. So were Shakespeare and Milton, and standard translations of the Greek and Roman classics, particularly Plutarch's *Lives*. Current English writers, especially Byron and Scott, were exceedingly popular. Local publishers felt free to reprint any current English author because there was no copyright law to protect him and hence English reprints were more attractive to them than the works of Americans.[47]

Every newspaper printing plant was a potential book publishing house, and frontier papers brought out an incredible number of works ranging from almanacs to legal statutes. Textbooks were perhaps the commonest books published by the local printing offices, but not infrequently a backwoods editor would bring out an English classic, ancient or modern, as his fancy chose, for no copyright deterred him. Cincinnati early took the lead as a publishing center. Schoolbooks and religious works poured off the little presses during the first three decades of settlement. Before the middle of the nineteenth century printing and publishing had become one of Cincinnati's great industries. Publishing also brought men of letters to the town and established Cincinnati's reputation for cultural enlightenment.

Subscription libraries helped in the dissemination of literature in the Ohio Valley. The first one recorded was set up in 1796 at Belpre, near Marietta. Subscribers took shares of stock at $10 per share and were entitled to draw out books provided the value of the books did not exceed the value of the stock. Amos Dunham, who came to the region in 1802, has left an account of the benefits of this library. "The long winter evenings were rather tedious," he wrote, "and in order to make them pass more smoothly, I purchased an interest in the Belpre Library, six miles distant. . . . Many a night have I passed in this manner (using pine knots in place of candles) till twelve or one o'clock, reading to my wife, while she was patcheling, carding, or spinning." [48] Among the books which Amos Dunham might have read to his busy wife were Locke's *Essay Concerning Human Understanding*, Gibbon's *Decline and Fall of the Roman Empire*, Goldsmith's *A History of the Earth, and Animated Nature*, Robertson's *History of Scotland*, Dr. Johnson's *Lives of the Poets*, and Hume's *History of England*—all solid substantial works.

Other libraries followed. The one most often mentioned is the famous "coonskin" library begun in 1803 in Ames Township, Athens County, Ohio, by book-hungry citizens who had no money but plenty of coon-skins. One of their number, Samuel Brown, loaded a wagon with skins and set out for Boston where he traded his furs for $73.50 worth of books including Harris' *Encyclopedia,* Goldsmith's *Works,* Robertson's *North America,* Ramsey's *American Revolution,* a few sermons and theological works, and some lighter reading matter such as *Children of the Abbey,* Fanny Burney's *Evelina,* and a play, *The London Merchant.* Later purchases included Locke's *Essays,* Shakespeare's *Works,* Plutarch's *Lives, Don Quixote, The Wealth of Nations,* Josephus' *History of the Jews,* and the early works of Walter Scott. One youth, Thomas Ewing, who contributed ten coonskins to the venture, is said to have taken books to the fields to read to the men laboring there.[49]

Even so small a settlement as Dayton in 1805 organized a Library Society and kept the books in the post office. Readers drew lots for the first glimpse at a new book and were fined three cents if they let candle grease drop on a page. Before 1812 probably a dozen subscription libraries were operating in Ohio. In Indiana, the Vincennes Library Company opened in 1808 with 210 volumes, for the most part history, geography, biography, and poetry.[50] Some of the early libraries quickly grew into respectable proportions. Within a year after it opened in 1814, the Cincinnati Circulating Library was in what Daniel Drake proudly called a "flourishing condition" with 800 volumes distributed over the whole field of knowledge including medicine and science.[51] Though only a small proportion of the total number of settlers in the West had access to such libraries, those who did served as carriers of the literary tradition.

The reading of English books, whether Shakespeare, the more recent works of eighteenth-century writers, or the latest thing from the pen of Byron or Scott, all helped to turn the mind of the frontiersman back eastward for his literary inspiration and knowledge. Even such entertainments as the theatre and many of the public lectures that he heard furthered his interest in English drama and English poetry. Traveling elocutionists recited speeches from Shakespeare, selections from Scott's poetry, or some other moving piece from an English author. When a traveling waxworks museum opened its show in Cincinnati in 1815, included in the scenes—along with George Washington, Aaron Burr, and the Prophet Elijah—was a tableau depicting Hamlet "the Prince of Denmark and the beautiful Ophelia." [52] To even a Western audience Hamlet and Ophelia were old friends.

With the exception of Cincinnati, the theatre did not flourish in the Northwest Territory as luxuriantly as it did in the Kentucky towns. Geography was against it, and professional traveling companies had great difficulty reaching the interior. Furthermore religious opposition was stronger. But "Thespian Societies" of amateurs occasionally gave performances, and now and then strolling players came to town. Cincinnati, however, on the professional circuit which included Lexington, Louisville, and St. Louis, became an important theatrical town. Of all the dramatists, Shakespeare enjoyed the greatest popularity, and more Shakespearean plays were performed in Cincinnati than in any other town except Louisville.[53] Dramatizations of Scott were sometimes given; Byron's *Mazeppa* with a live horse on the stage proved an attraction which was to grow in popularity in the later West; and Goldsmith's *She Stoops to Conquer* and the plays of George Colman the Younger were also favorites. Only Kotzebue's *Pizarro* approached the English dramatists in popularity.

As a self-conscious literature developed in the West, professional writers like Timothy Flint and James Hall complained about the literary subservience to Great Britain. They established magazines and appealed to Western writers—as well as to Western subscribers—to support American literature, which, they assured their readers, was just as good as anything being written in Great Britain. But Americans perversely kept buying British books and even British quarterlies. And American publishers, deterred by no copyright, provided cheap reprints for the trade. This literary piracy was one cause for the bitter commentary heaped upon the United States by Dickens and some other British travelers.

The West, however, did produce an enormous body of writing, not much of which survived. Professor Ralph Leslie Rusk's two-volume *Literature of the Middle-Western Frontier* provides an index to the literary aspi-

rations of the region and supplies clues which ought
to lead to further interpretation of the culture of the
West as reflected in some of these writers.

Timothy Flint, missionary and traveler, wrote sentimental novels which are no longer read, but his
*Recollections of the Last Ten Years . . . in the Valley
of the Mississippi* (1826) has had a modern edition and
is still an entertaining document. His romanticized
Biographical Memoir of Daniel Boone, published in
Cincinnati in 1833, went through fourteen editions and
gave to the world the conventional notion of that
worthy. James Hall, lawyer, politician, and editor,
became a vocal defender of things Western. His duties,
first as judge in Illinois and later as state treasurer, did
not prevent his writing poetry, fiction, and essays, and
editing the *Illinois Intelligencer.* Perhaps his best known
works today are *Legends of the West* (1832) and
Sketches of History, Life, and Manners of the West
(2 vols., 1834-35). Both Flint and Hall did their best
to encourage Western writers and to appeal to national
patriotism to support the native literature. But what
they did not perceive was that they themselves were
also merely imitators of conventional literary patterns
inherited from British literature. Though Flint was
much under the influence of French romanticism, and
of Chateaubriand in particular, he never broke away
from British models. Far from being emancipated by
the "freedom" of a new country, most writers on the
Middle Western frontier clung tenaciously to accepted

forms and appear to have been influenced even in the content of their work by the inherited tradition. They frequently saw what it was conventional to see.

In discussing the effect of the wilderness on Sally Hastings, a woman who made a journey to the wilds of Western Pennsylvania in 1800 and wrote in both prose and verse, Professor Leon Howard has wisely observed that among writers on the frontier "conventional modes of expression were probably maintained with a rigidity not found among equally sensitive people in a more civilized environment." And he adds that "timeless Bostonians who submitted verses to early Ohio newspapers were not necessarily producing poems through which we might study the influence of the frontier." [54] If anything, the crudities of the frontier made the self-conscious writer more eager than ever to retain the patterns that were evidence of a cultivated style. With Professor Rusk's compilation of writers and Professor Howard's suggestions of a method, students might profitably take a second look at the men who were trying to bring literary culture to the West.

It would have been a miracle, indeed, if Western writers and the conscious apostles of civilization had brought any large stock of original ideas. The force of the past was too strong. While they looked forward to a new land of opportunity, they also looked back to a land which for centuries had been the source of law, literature, learning, manners, and morality. If they were not to become mere woods people, they would have to preserve the best of that civilized past.

FOUR

Culture and Anarchy on the Pacific Coast: The Age of Gold

THOMAS JEFFERSON had dreamed of linking the Pacific Coast to the Anglo-Saxon East in a great American Empire populated by people like those who had settled the Atlantic seaboard. As the Children of Israel had sent spies into the Promised Land, so Jefferson sent Lewis and Clark to report on the country from the Mississippi to the sea. The reports which they brought back fell on fertile soil. During the years when the Ohio Valley and the eastern side of the Mississippi were gradually settling down into a civilized way of life, the interest in the West beyond the Mississippi, and farther still beyond the mountains, was growing. American trappers and fur traders, indomitable mountain men, had found trails down the most distant western rivers to the Pacific coast.[1] Newspaper editors and politicians were beginning to talk about the Manifest Destiny of Americans to occupy all of the continent between the two oceans. Manifest Destiny was an Anglo-Saxon concept. As the papers and politicians defined it, Manifest Destiny was the divine right of one-hundred-percent Americans, meaning Anglo-Saxon Americans, or those who had been thoroughly assimilated into the Anglo-Saxon pattern, to occupy this land.[2] "Foreigners," except by a special concession of the elect, were not divinely appointed to have a part in it.

During the 1830's and '40's, adventurous emigrants and missionaries began a steady push to the West which would not end until all the country was peopled by citizens of the United States. The Kentucky and Ohio regions were filling up and some of the settlers there were getting restless to move on to fresher, cheaper, or better land. Always the country beyond beckoned. The pressure from the Atlantic seaboard continued. New England was a hive which constantly produced new swarms. New York, Pennsylvania, Virginia, and the Carolinas contributed their numbers. The great panic of 1837 ruined many a citizen, townspeople as well as farmers, and made them so despondent over conditions at home that they were ready to seek a new life on the prairies of Indiana, Illinois, or even farther west in Iowa. Some began to move into Michigan, Wisconsin, and Minnesota. Adventurous Southerners and a few New Englanders had already pushed down into the Southwest and formed an Anglo-Saxon enclave in Texas. By 1835 they felt strong and righteous enough to rebel against the Mexicans and set up a republic which would soon become a part of the United States. The far Northwest also felt the impact of Atlantic-seaboard Americans. In the autumn of 1834, Jason Lee and a party of Methodist missionaries arrived overland at Fort Vancouver in Oregon and accepted the hospitality of the Hudson's Bay Company. They established a mission in the Willamette Valley which was soon thriving. In 1836, Dr. Marcus Whitman, a Presbyterian medical missionary, and Henry Spalding, a Congregationalist preacher, came overland with their wives and established a mission near Walla Walla. If the missionaries had been real estate promoters, their descriptions of the fertility of the valleys and the wholesomeness of the climate could not have been more seductive. Soon the Willamette Valley was teeming with American farmers. American expansionists would increase the pressure for the settlement of the vexed Oregon boundary question. Finally under President Polk, war with Mexico and negotiation with England gave the United States the whole territory between the Atlantic and the Pacific to become a great inland empire.

On the afternoon of January 24, 1848 an event occurred which suddenly shifted interest from the prairies and plains of the interior of America, from the rich valleys of the Northwest, and from the grazing lands of Texas to California. On that afternoon, James W. Marshall, just completing a sawmill for John A. Sutter on the South Fork of the American River, took from the millrace a few yellow flakes that looked like gold.[3] Few discoveries have had such a violent impact on the imagination of the world. The greed for gold, always endemic, burst out as a violent fever which swept North and South America, Europe, Australia, the Hawaiian Islands, and the coast of China. For Marshall and Sutter, try as they might, could not keep their discovery secret. The news spread slowly at first, to

Monterey, to San José, to San Francisco, and at last to the sleepy settlements around the ranchos and missions in the South. But soon the rumor of gold was drawing men like a magnet to the mountain valleys of the north. The first to arrive easily picked nuggets and flakes of pure gold out of the sand and rifts in the rock. Newspapers in the East reported the gold strike and within a few months eager men in Great Britain, Holland, France, Germany, and the countries of South America were dreaming of riches which they hoped to find in California. Rarely in history had such a stream of emigration been concentrated upon one region.

Gold-seekers swarmed out from the East. The towns along the Mississippi filled with emigrants preparing to strike across the plains for the golden West. St. Louis, long a point of departure for the Santa Fe trail, swelled in importance. St. Joseph on the Missouri became a great outfitting point for emigrants headed for the Platte River-South Pass route to the gold fields. Wagon trains lumbered across the plains and deserts in an endless stream. Many tried to reach California by sea, some by crossing the Isthmus of Panama and transshipping on the other side, some by going the long way around Cape Horn. Ships from Europe, from Australia, and from the east and west coasts of South America, dropped passengers and cargo at San Francisco. These vessels frequently lost their crews who jumped ship and headed for the mines. Ships were reported riding at anchor with only a cat on board. Everybody else had gone to the hills. Monterey and the other settled places of California lost their populations as the inhabitants caught the gold fever. Old men, women, and children struggled along with able-bodied men on their way to El Dorado. Nothing like it had ever been seen.

Within two years after the discovery of gold, the population of California swelled from 15,000 to 93,000 and two years later, in 1852, the state claimed more than 260,000 people concentrated chiefly in the north central portion with San Francisco as the metropolis.[4] Towns grew up overnight, towns of nothing except tents and rough shacks. Sometimes they would be deserted as suddenly as they had grown by the rumor of richer strikes in some other valley. The volatile population drifted and probed streams and valleys throughout central California. A story was told to illustrate the power of rumor. St. Peter, it was said, had been disturbed by miners who got to heaven and dug up the golden streets. To get rid of them, he called one of the most responsible in the lot and persuaded him to spread a story that there had been a gold strike in hell. The next morning all the miners were waiting at the gate to begin an emigration to hell, with the man who had circulated the story the first in line. "What are you doing here?" St. Peter asked. "Well, St. Peter," he replied, "you can't be sure we won't make a better strike down there." Many of the California immigrants found gold; some found enough to make them rich; others, the eternal victims of bad luck, had only hard labor and misery as their reward.

The development of the California frontier was like

no other in previous American history. Its growth was sudden and its elements were more varied and explosive than any other frontier region had ever seen. For the first time, the British stock, meaning the native American people from the Atlantic seaboard, had serious competition from other types. California had, of course, been Spanish, but the early Spanish and mission culture had spread thin leaving only a residue of a few families, place names, legends, and a pretext for fiesta days sponsored in later times by romantic chambers of commerce. The gold rush, however, brought many more Latin Americans, from Mexico, Chile, Argentina, and elsewhere in South America. It also brought Frenchmen, Germans, and other Continental Europeans. For the first time it introduced Asiatic and Pacific island types in the Chinese and Polynesians who found their way to the Coast. Everybody, speaking all the languages of the world, it seemed, had come in search of gold. The kind of civilization which developed would depend on the vigor of the dominant groups.

From the first there was friction between what we shall call, for want of a better term, the Anglo-Saxon or "American" stock, and the Latins and Asiatics. Though some of the Spanish people antedated the recent arrivals from the Atlantic states, the "Americans" looked down upon them as "foreigners" and interlopers. The mining camps saw frequent riots as Americans attempted to drive out Mexicans, Chileans, and others whom they disliked. Part of the trouble, to be sure, was economic competition, but the animosities lay deeper than that, and it was symbolic of the provincialism, as well as the vigorous determination, of the American stock to claim the country as its own and to make it over in the image of other American communities. Where opposition was strong, as in California, the hostilities were all the more violent. In nearly every mining camp, the Americans tried to drive out the Latin foreigners, and these included the French. For some curious reason, possibly because they were less numerous, Nordic people usually escaped the violence directed toward other foreigners. In the mining town of Sonora in 1850, the American miners rioted and attempted to drive out the Latins. This was only one episode out of many. The Americans openly declared that they alone were appointed of God to reap the benefits of California's wealth and held mass meetings to denounce Spaniards and all other non-English-speaking rogues. The first legislature of 1850 passed the "Foreign Miners' Tax Law" providing among other things a license costing $30 per month payable by all outlanders.[5] This law had to be modified by the next legislature, but it was indicative of the mood of the Americans who filled their resolutions and speeches with cant phrases about their divine right to the natural wealth of the state.

Foreigners got scant justice, of course, either from the extralegal tribunals of the mining camps or from lawfully appointed judges and juries. It was conventional to attribute most of the crimes and violence to "Mexicans" or more vaguely to "foreigners." Lynch law and riots frequently made life hazardous for foreigners, male or female. When a Spanish-American woman stabbed to death a drunken American who stumbled into her house and insulted her at Downieville in July, 1851, the furious crowd demanded her life and that of her Latin lover. Cries of "Hang them" showed the temper of the community, but some more judicial than the others took up the cry, "Give them a fair trial and then hang them." That comported with Anglo-Saxon notions of justice. She was presently hanged.[6] When a naturalized Irishman was stabbed by a Spaniard at Rich Bar in August, 1852, a similar scene occurred. "Down with the Spaniards!" "Drive every foreigner off the river!" "Oh, if you have a drop of American blood in your veins, it must cry out for vengeance upon the cowardly assassins of poor Tom," these were the calls to the riot that followed.[7]

Americans expressed dislike of the gregarious habits of French miners and the disorganized and slovenly way that Spanish and South-American miners operated. The foreigners were different; they were in the way; and they were bad. Every foreigner was suspect. "He had no business, as an alien, to come to the land that God had given us," is the ironic observation of Josiah Royce. "And if he was a native Californian, a born 'greaser,' then so much the worse for him. He was so much the more our born foe; we hated his whole degenerate, thieving, landowning, lazy, and discontented race. Some of them were now even bandits; most of them by this time were, with our help, more or less drunkards; and it was not our fault if they were not all rascals! So they deserved no better." [8] The anti-foreign attitude of Americans in California during the gold rush, and later, deserves careful analysis, for it illustrates dramatically a significant nativistic quality which has persisted in American character and flourished with remarkable vigor in the Far West. The "old Americans," meaning the Atlantic stock assimilated into the British tradition, have been regarded as God's elect. Chauvinistic patriotism, especially in the West, has glorified this element in American life. Ironically, this glorification has come with special force in communities which owed much of their development to others.

The immigrants from the eastern United States who took over California had no thought except to Americanize it. To have adapted themselves to such Spanish culture as they found would have been regarded as too heretical to be considered. When the first legislature met to consider laws for the new commonwealth, it adopted on April 13, 1850 a statute which had far-reaching implications because of its connections with the distant past of English tradition as well as its forecast of the future philosophy of law. It read: "The common law of England, so far as it is not repugnant to or inconsistent with the Constitution of the United States, or the constitution or laws of this state, is the rule of decision in all the courts of this state." [9]

The hell-roaring life in the mining camps and boom towns of California has been the aspect most emphasized in fiction and legend. When Western towns celebrate "frontier days," the citizens grow whiskers, affect a swagger, and try to recover some of the alleged glamor of the riotous life that went on in the bars and dance halls of earlier times. Rarely does anyone recall the sober efforts of men and women, even in the beginning, to reproduce the civilized patterns of behavior. Violent, boisterous, and untrammeled as was life, there was also another side. The anarchistic and disintegrating forces of the frontier met another force less violent but eternally steady in its pressure: the determination of a few persistent men and women to re-create in the wilderness a stable social order with its traditional amenities. This conflict between anarchy and civilization was not spectacular; its battles were not often sufficiently dramatic to become the theme of ballad, novel, or movie. But the struggle was clearly defined and men could see what was happening. It was not a conflict left to chance. The forces of civilization were constantly planning campaigns and waging war in new places. Indeed, the struggle continues, for California is a land of many frontiers, from the gold-rush days to the present day. It remains a land of Canaan into which settlers are still pouring, trying to adjust themselves to a new life, and hoping to discover a better or at least a more comfortable existence.

From a village in eastern Iowa, on the last day of April, 1849, a little family set out in a covered wagon for the gold fields. It was much like hundreds of other families headed in the same direction. The wagon was drawn by three yokes of oxen, and inside were a young

mother and father and a two-year-old daughter. The
mother had been born at Stratford-on-Avon; the father
also in England, in Rutlandshire. Both had come to
America as children, been brought up in the East, and
now were heading West in search of their fortunes. No
one would have said that they held any greater significance for California than any one of the thousands of
others who had turned their eyes toward the Golden
Gate. Yet they did. They represented the quiet, determined people who would translate California from wild
lawlessness to orderly civility. They were Josiah and
Sarah Royce, and they would become the parents of a
son, also named Josiah. He became a teacher, historian,
and philosopher and ended his career as a distinguished
professor at Harvard.

Mrs. Royce kept a journal, one of the most moving
accounts of the hardships of the journey to the West
and of life in the crude towns of California. She carried
with her a Bible and one or two other books. And she
was soon teaching the children of the settlements.
Josiah Royce was later to describe the influence of hearing the Bible read to him by his mother and the fascination of the stories which were a part of his education,
as they were a part of the education of many other
Californians. When the Royces settled for a time in a
mining camp near Sacramento, Mrs. Royce got together
a few books and a small organ, and set aside one room
of her canvas shack as a "parlor." "But the parlor—
that was my pride," she reports. "There was against
the wall, a small table, covered with a cloth, and hold-

ing a knick-knack or two, and a few choice books. Above it was a narrow shelf with some other books, and some papers. . . . But the pride of all was my melodeon. . . . There was little time for music during the day, except on Sundays; but at night when the children were all in bed, and the store—for we had a store again—kept my husband away, I used often to indulge myself in the melodies and harmonies that brought to me the most precious memories of earth, and opened up visions of heaven. And then those bare rafters and cloth walls became for the time a banquet-hall, a cathedral." [10] With books and music, civilization was on the way. When the Royces were finally established in Grass Valley, Mrs. Royce taught school and brought her influence to bear on the whole district.

The Royces were not isolated phenomena. They were not alone among rioting hordes of drunken miners, as one is likely to believe from reading some of the accounts of the diggings. When a soft-spoken young man stopped to admire little Mary, Mrs. Royce discovered that he was a physician who had come to make his fortune digging gold. For partners he had a well-educated lawyer and a geologist. "I soon found," says Mrs. Royce, "that this was by no means a solitary instance. But a much larger number of the miners belonged to other very valuable classes of society. Merchants, mechanics, farmers were all there in large numbers. So that in almost every mining camp there was enough of the element of order, to control, or very much influence, the opposite forces." [11]

One of the many things that made the California frontier different was the large number of educated men who gave up professions in the East and came West under the excitement of the gold fever. Lawyers, doctors, teachers, university professors, preachers, and business men were not uncommon in the diggings— not in their professional occupations but in some more lucrative capacity. "Professor Shepard from one of the first institutions in the states is driving a cart from Sacramento city to the mines, from which he is coining a mint of money," a Maine woman wrote back from San Francisco in September 1849. "Everyone must do something; it matters but very little what it is, if they stick to it, they are bound to make money." [12] The writer of this letter, the wife of a doctor, herself was doing very well running a boarding house. Among her guests were two schoolmarms from the East, one of whom had her eyes on matrimony as the surest way to economic success. Another correspondent, also the wife of a doctor, described the kind of people who made up the population of the wild mining village of Indian Bar in 1852: "Of the Americans, the majority are of the better class of mechanics. Next to these, in number, are the sailors and the farmers. There are a few merchants and steamboat-clerks, three or four physicians, and one lawyer. We have no ministers, though fourteen miles from here there is a 'Rancho,' kept by a man of distinguished appearance, an accomplished monte-dealer and horse-jockey, who is *said* to have been—in the States—a preacher of the Gospel. I know not if this be true; but at any rate, such things are not uncommon in California." [13]

The story of the preacher turned gambler crops up here and there in the California legend, but actually most of the preachers as well as other professional men remained true to the ethics of their callings, even if they did take a fling at mining. After the first mad rush was over, the wisest men discovered that it was more profitable—and easier—to leave mining to those accustomed to such labor and to turn to vocations more in keeping with their own talents. The primitive society of the mining camps swiftly altered before the normal divisions of labor.

The iniquity and the prosperity of the gold rush towns were alike a challenge to Protestant preachers of all denominations who came in amazing numbers. The same ships which brought their quotas of gamblers and women of easy virtue also had aboard preachers, ready and eager to do battle with the minions of the devil whom they had no difficulty identifying. California had a long tradition of Catholic missions, but if the missions had been prepared to minister to the spiritual needs of the newcomers, the prejudices of the hordes from the East would have thwarted them, for the vast majority of the incoming Americans were Protestant in background, however remote from their daily activities religion might be. Even before the gold rush, Methodists from the Oregon mission had begun to look upon California as a fertile field, and Methodist services are recorded in San Francisco as early as 1847. In April of that year, a Methodist missionary bound for Oregon, William Roberts, came ashore in San Francisco to investigate the prospects for a Methodist mission there. He preached in the dining room of Brown's Hotel, with a bar on one side and gambling tables on the other, but he held his congregation. One sailor was so pleased that he put a five-dollar gold piece in the collection and remarked to Roberts that he had preached "a damned good sermon." [14] Other Methodist preachers followed. In the spring of 1849, the Methodists were holding services in a blue tent on Powell Street, and by September William Taylor had arrived by ship from New York with materials for a church building stored in the hold. Lumber was scarce and costly. A cynic tried to persuade him that San Francisco was not ready for a church and he would do better to sell the materials for ten thousand dollars and try religion in some other territory.[15] But the Methodists were there to stay and their preachers were soon exhorting sinners throughout the mining country.

The earliest systematic onslaught against sin waged by the Protestants in San Francisco was a communal enterprise. The "better element" in the town, concerned over the wickedness of their city, on November 2, 1849, appointed as "city chaplain" Timothy Dwight Hunt, lately arrived from the mission field in Hawaii. His experience with sin in Honolulu, it was believed, eminently fitted him to deal with the problems of San Francisco. He was a Congregationalist by conviction but technically at this time a New School Presbyterian.

Joining in the common effort were Methodists, Baptists, Presbyterians, Congregationalists, Episcopalians, and Mormons. Encouragement in the form of a promise of gold dust to add to his salary came from Samuel Brannan, a Mormon elder who soon made a fortune in the town. For a time, the Protestants worked in blissful harmony, if we may believe Hunt's words: "There was sweet pleasure in the fact of our unity in diversity. Our gatherings in Sabbath congregations and in Sabbath school and Prayer Meeting, or in the social circle, were those of one family of believers, in each of whom we recognized the common Master." [16] So confident were these workers in the vineyard that on New Year's Eve they gathered to hold a union prayer service for the conversion of the world. California was already taking a large view of its responsibilities.

But the co-ordination of activity under Mr. Hunt's city chaplaincy did not mean that the individual denominations were idle. Each was busy about the Lord's work according to its own doctrines. The Baptists first held services during the winter of 1849 in the home of a merchant, C. L. Ross, where the pastor, O. C. Wheeler, organized a Sunday School. By August 5 of that year they had bought a ten-thousand-dollar lot and erected a six-thousand-dollar church building, said to have been the first permanent Protestant church building in California.[17] Under the ministry of Albert Williams, who arrived on the steamer "Oregon" on April 1, 1839, the Presbyterians quickly organized a church and began a search for the elect. The question of the priority of the Methodists and Presbyterians, and of the relation of "Old School" and "New School" Presbyterians to each other and to the Congregationalists, who were also early in the field, has vexed historians of the Protestant faiths in California.[18] The important thing for us to remember is that they were all intensely busy. Even the Episcopalians, inactive on the Middle-Western frontier, bestirred themselves with unwonted zeal. By the end of 1849, the Methodists, Baptists, Presbyterians, Episcopalians, and Congregationalists all had organized churches, and the Episcopalians had a second church in the process of organization.[19] Clearly San Francisco was going to be a rich city, able to support Christian enterprise. Ships coming into San Francisco Bay brought preachers loaded with Bibles, hymn books, catechisms, and tracts. They swarmed out of San Francisco to the mines and to the new towns a-building, where they raised money for churches. The godless were not going to damnation unwarned. Someone later observed that California had more churches and less religion than any state in the Union. However that may be, the preachers of frontier days were valiantly doing battle to drive the devil to cover and to build sanctuaries against his return.

All of the Protestant sects which took a lead in seeking California's salvation were deeply concerned about fostering education on all levels but especially in establishing colleges. Hundreds of colleges throughout the nation date from these years. Those sects which at first had been contemptuous of higher learning were now

active in demanding colleges and in promoting legislation for public schools. Education as a way to both
social and spiritual salvation had become an article of
faith with countless Americans. The California frontier opened wide new educational opportunities, and
religious groups hastened to seize them.

But before colleges could be founded, it was necessary to provide for elementary education. We sometimes forget that a considerable number of the gold-
seekers brought their wives with them, and that the
education of their children was a difficult problem. The
missionary preachers helped solve it by opening little
schools in their homes and churches. One of the earliest
zealots for schools was a Baptist layman, John C. Pelton, of Andover, Massachusetts, who came around the
Horn from Boston in the autumn of 1849. Instead of
mining equipment, he brought a shipment of school
supplies. Lashed to the mast of the ship was a school
bell which bore the inscription, "Presented to the First
Free Grammar School of San Francisco by the Henry
W. Hooper Co., Boston, Massachusetts." Though Pelton
had very little money himself, he procured subscriptions
from interested citizens and in December opened a
free school in the Baptist Church. His was the first
school which made no tuition charge.[20]

Many of the missionary preachers combined school
teaching with their spiritual vocations. One of the first
ministers sent out by the American Home Missionary
Society was S. H. Willey, who for a time taught a
school in the town hall at Monterey. This building,

designed in part for a school, had been the special care of the ex-naval chaplain, W. R. Colton, who served as alcalde of Monterey. Fines from gamblers were designated as a fund for a school, and Colton was diligent in raiding gambling parties for the cause.

Though preachers were often willing to teach school, they could not take care of the increasing needs. In 1853 at a May Day celebration in San Francisco, nearly a thousand school children marched in a parade. "Each one carried flowers," says one account of the event, "and the sight was a pleasant one for San Franciscans, although it was by no means the first time that homeless men had been reminded of the presence of happy homes in their midst." [21] To educate the happy children some more systematic plan for schools had to be devised.

The state was slow to provide adequately for schools. Though the Constitution of 1849 had recognized the need and set aside state land for educational purposes, nothing much was done to establish schools. The first governor did not mention education in his message to the legislature. Not until 1852 did the state legislature levy any general tax for schools. The tax law provided that no money should be allocated to denominational or sectarian schools, but this was changed the following year to permit schools run by religious organizations to share in the state funds. Certain of the sterner Protestants objected to the law when they realized that Catholic parochial schools were benefiting, and they succeeded in 1855 in having the law repealed.

Though newspapers demanded better schools, taxes remained inadequate. In 1859 the State Superintendent of Public Instruction declared that "our present school system has furnished instruction to only 11,183 children out of 40,530; and to them for only five and a half months out of the twelve. . . . If we do not take instant and effective means to remedy it these 29,347 neglected children will grow up into 29,347 benighted men and women—a number nearly sufficient at ordinary times to control the vote of the state, and in consequence to shape its legislation and its destiny." [22] The legislature did not take "instant" measures of relief, and the 29,347 unfortunate ignoramuses were well along the road to maturity before the state's conscience troubled it. A later Superintendent of Public Instruction, a zealous New Hampshire Yankee named John Swett, in 1864 declared that California more than any other state needed a good school system if her citizens were to be assimilated into the traditional culture, and John Swett was horrified at the thought that Californians might not become as much as possible like New Englanders. "Her [California's] population is drawn from all nations," he pointed out. "The next generation will be a composite one, made up of the heterogeneous atoms of all nationalities. Nothing can Americanize these chaotic elements and breathe into them the spirit of our institutions but the public schools." [23] By 1866 legislation had provided a satisfactory public school system, but the campaign had been long and hard. Many Californians were still too concerned with the materialistic pursuit of wealth to care much about the future welfare of the commonwealth. To the usual conflict on the frontier between barbarism and enlightenment, California had added an unusual concentration upon the mere materialistic. A part of the trouble was the general spirit of the times, the crassness of what Mark Twain called the "Gilded Age," but California had more than its share of disdain of everything except the material. Upon this hard and rocky obstacle the soldiers of enlightenment would shatter many a lance during the frontier period and later.

If the opponents of cultural advancement were obdurate, so were the apostles of enlightenment. Rarely has a state seen more determined folk than those who established California's institutions of higher learning in the two decades following the gold rush. Not only did they found academies, colleges, and universities, but they made them institutions dedicated to traditional learning in spite of the indifference or even the active clamor for mere vocational training. The battle was no minor engagement, and the victory did not stay comfortably won; even yet the lines of battle remain drawn, not only in California, but throughout the nation.

Higher education in the first two decades of American California was regarded as the special responsibility of religious groups. Nearly every important denomination or sect set about founding private schools, academies, and colleges. Especially active were the Methodists, the Presbyterians, and the Congregationalists. The Catholics, who had been first on the ground, soon were also busy opening up convents, academies, and colleges. By the beginning of the third decade they had thirteen convents and academies and five colleges.[24] The activity of the Catholics in education stimulated the Protestants enormously. On no other previous frontier had evangelical Protestantism faced such serious competition for the minds and souls of young people. No one can say which exerted the greater stimulus, the zeal for pure learning or the fear of Catholic domination, but whatever the cause, Protestants never showed greater fervor in the cause of education.

One of the first acts of the organized Methodist church in California was to project a university. The instructions given the earliest Methodist missionaries included the establishment of an institution of higher learning, and at a conference in San José on January 6, 1851 clergy and laymen agreed to proceed at once to found a school "of the grade of a university." [25] The following July, California Wesleyan University was chartered, but a month later the name was changed to the more high-sounding University of the Pacific. Its site was also moved in 1852 from San José to Santa Clara. With only a handful of teachers, the University of the Pacific set about providing the essentials of a classical education modified by Methodist doctrine. One of its influential leaders in the early period was Isaac Owen, himself a product of the frontier but one imbued with a desire to make available the resources of ancient knowledge which he had had to dig out for himself. A semi-literate blacksmith in his early manhood, he was chiefly self-educated and became one of the most earnest advocates of learning. He was also one of the most successful money-raisers for education in his day. Before coming to California he had been financial agent for Asbury University in Indiana. After observing the opportunities in California, he remarked that he would like to see "a high school at every crossroad and a college in every county." [26] He traveled with a copy of Hume's *History of England* and a New Testament in Greek in his saddlebags, and he commended the reading of history and the study of Greek to preachers and laymen alike. Isaac Owen typified the zeal for college education that was characteristic of evangelical Protestantism in this period.

While the Methodists were busy starting the University of the Pacific (changed in 1911 to the College of the Pacific), other denominations were also active. Within a decade the Protestants in California had projected eight colleges. Some died but others continued in one form or another to the present day. One of the most interesting projects in the light of later events was technically non-denominational but in reality New School Presbyterian and Congregational in inspiration. That was the establishment of the College of California, which had so much to do with the development of the University of California.

Three Presbyterian and Congregational ministers had met at Sacramento in October, 1849, and talked about California's need for a college. One of these men was S. H. Willey, a minister sent out by the Home Missionary Society, and a graduate of Dartmouth and Union Theological Seminary. Willey became an ardent advocate of college education. Two years later, in May, 1853, San Francisco received another apostle of education, Henry Durant, Congregational minister and graduate of Yale. He had come expressly to start some kind of seminary of learning. Willey and Durant joined forces and with the help of other Presbyterian and Congregational ministers and laymen, they established Contra Costa Academy in Oakland. Within two years, in 1855, this school received a charter as the College of California. Though the principal supporters were Congregationalists and Presbyterians, it was theoretically a non-sectarian college devoted to the liberal arts. Not until 1864 did the college graduate a class; at commencement in that year the Governor made a great oration describing these graduates as the "advance-guard of the California division of learning, [the] pioneer corps of the battalion of her scholars." The College of California had in the meantime acquired land a few miles to the north overlooking the Bay and was planning to move from Oakland as soon as buildings could be erected.

While earnest church folk were attempting to create in the College of California an "institution . . . to furnish the means of a thorough and comprehensive education under the pervading spirit and influence of the Christian religion," [27] other more secular people were agitating for a state university. A fight between religious interests, who stood for the liberal arts tradition, and non-religious elements, who were eager to promote "practical" and vocational training, was shaping up. The Superintendent of Public Instruction, Andrew J. Moulder, in 1858 advocated a California version of West Point as the ideal form of state institution of higher learning. He pointed out that Virginia Military Institute and the Citadel in South Carolina provided military leaders and well-trained engineers, the kind of men useful to a new state on the fringes of civilization. The idea was appealing to many practical men who believed that a good surveyor would be infinitely more useful than another parson able to read the Greek New Testament. Others were clamoring for a school of mining and an agricultural college. The classic conflict which has raged from that day to this over the purpose and functions of education had begun.

The advocates of practical training in a state university were up against an inspired opposition skilled in the arts of persuasion. An unexpected opponent of state training appeared in 1856 in the person of Horace Bushnell, a Congregational preacher from Connecticut, who had come to California for his health and saw an opportunity to strike a blow for learning and the Lord, the two being more or less co-ordinate in his thinking. He allied himself with the supporters of the College of California and made an appeal to the state to rally in its behalf and forget about a state university, especially one devoted to vocational training. In a pamphlet and in the newspapers he declared that state universities could not succeed, that faculties of such institutions would be as subservient to politics as the lowliest constable in fear of his job, and that a state university would merely create political patronage without advancing learning.[28] To avoid this sad condition Bushnell urged the state to back the College of California.

The eloquence of the Reverend Mr. Bushnell was persuasive and it may have delayed the foundation of the state university a few years but it did not please everybody, even among other pious sectarians opposed to state education. The Old School Presbyterians, for example, complained violently about the domination of the College of California by Congregationalists and New School Presbyterians. The Reverend W. A. Scott in his monthly periodical, the *Expositor*, for February, 1861, asked rhetorically: "Who are the chief professors? Alumni of Yale College. What is the fashion, color, and shape of the College? Its professors and friends frequently boast that it is to be 'the Yale of the Pacific.' And is not Yale essentially a denominational, Congregational institution? . . . Are not almost all the letters which have been published in favor of the school from New England men who are themselves connected with Congregational institutions, or from such as are known to be high church sectarians?"[29] Scott had come from New Orleans and was obviously fed up with New England pretensions to being the fountainhead of all worth-while learning. He did not wish to give any comfort to the proponents of a state university, but he did want something closer to his kind of Presbyterianism than the College of California.

Despite its claim to being non-sectarian the College of California did not receive adequate support and it looked hopefully to the state government for help. When the agitation for a college of mines and agriculture was acute, it established a department of science in San Francisco and labeled it a "Mining and Agricultural College." Then it applied to the legislature for support of its whole educational enterprise. The state was in no mood to support a religious institution and would have none of it. But the College of California was unwilling to sit by and watch the state give its money to a strictly vocational institution. It began one of the shrewdest propaganda campaigns in the history of California to persuade state officials and the public that education was broader than the techniques of mining and farming.

The commencement exercises at the College of California in 1867 marked the climax of the struggle for liberal learning as opposed to mere vocationalism. The exercises were carefully planned, and someone with a stroke of genius thought of inviting Benjamin Silliman, Jr., to give the address. Silliman, son of a distinguished scientist, was himself professor of chemistry and mineralogy at Yale. His eminence as a practical as well as a theoretical scientist was unquestioned. The topic of his address was "The Truly Practical Man Necessarily an Educated Man." With Governor Low sitting on the rostrum and many practical men and legislators in the audience, Silliman made an impassioned plea for the liberal arts as essential to the engineer and farmer as well as the parson and the teacher. He insisted that the so-called "practical man"—meaning the man without a broad liberal education—was necessarily the worst of theorists. He proved with examples the value of liberal studies in making scientists genuinely practical. And he shamed those whose ignorance and arrogance made them disdain sound learning in non-technical fields. Silliman also analyzed the plans of the proposed state college of agriculture, mining, and the mechanical arts and demonstrated that they fell short of providing adequate education even within their own frames of reference. This was doctrine which the advocates of a technological university had not expected to hear from one of the most eminent scientists in the nation. During the day other talks drove home the same ideas. Dr. Andrew L. Stone, a Congregational minister and an orator famous in the region, addressed the Associated Alumni—a group of graduates from many institutions— on the relation of the college to the state. Stone was a vigorous fighter in the cause. On an earlier occasion he had declared that "we want the College in the new young life of the State as a bond with the past. . . . The halls of liberal culture open backward into the galleries of antiquity and onward into the life of the present. . . . The College was wanted also to combat the materialism against which all new communities contend." [30] Before the day was over, Governor Low had expressed the wish that the College of California and the state might co-operate in the educational enterprise. [31] If the battle had not been won by liberal learning, at least the outer works had been stormed and taken.

By autumn the trustees of the College of California had received assurances that the State of California had no intention of restricting its support merely to technology, and on October 9, 1867 they voted to deed to the state their Oakland campus and their property a few miles to the north.

On March 23, 1868, the University of California received its charter and began instruction in September, 1869. The friends of liberal education received a jolt in November, 1868 when the new board of regents turned down Dr. Joseph Henry, able head of the Smithsonian Institution, and elected General George B. McClellan president. Protests throughout the state were violent. Eventually McClellan declined the offer and the regents elected Henry Durant, a clergyman and Greek scholar.

The site of the University received its name, Berkeley, in 1866 after prolonged discussion by the College of California. A committee at first suggested the name Peralta after the original owner of the land, but the College did not approve of a Spanish name. Finally one of the committee remembered the poetic stanza beginning "Westward the course of empire takes its way," and suggested the name of its author, George Berkeley, Bishop of Cloyne, as suitable for the college town. In this way, the site of the University of California came to have the name of an eighteenth-century English philosopher and divine.[32]

Like most universities in the West, the University of California from 1870 onward admitted women on an equal footing with men. Long before this date, the proper education of women had troubled Californians. Many Protestants had sent their daughters to Catholic convent schools or to the Catholic college of Notre Dame at San José. So good were the Catholic schools that Protestants became alarmed. An editorial in the *Pacific* for September 3, 1852 praised the excellence of Santa Clara College and the College of Notre Dame, and warned Protestants that they ought to make provision for the education of their daughters as well as their sons lest they be drawn away from the religion of their fathers.[33] The desire for a Protestant school led to the founding of the Benecia Seminary for Young Ladies in 1852, which in time developed into Mills College. The first teachers were two young women imported from Vermont, which was believed to be a fountain of pure religion and solid American culture. Two years after its establishment, Mary Atkins, a graduate of Oberlin, became principal. She was an emancipated woman who had taught in Ohio before setting out alone for California via the Isthmus of Panama, certainly no journey for a timid soul. Within a few years she owned Benecia Seminary and was turning out Protestant young ladies who could read Latin or argue about theology. A returned missionary from Hawaii, named Cyrus Mills bought the seminary from Miss Atkins in 1865 and later moved it to Oakland where it was called Mills Seminary. When Dr. and Mrs. Mills in 1877 deeded the institution to a board of trustees they expressed the hope that the school might develop into a college like Mt. Holyoke in Massachusetts.[34]

The desire of educators on the Pacific Coast was not for originality but for as close a duplication as possible of educational institutions in the East. The New England influence was especially strong and persisted for many years. During the land boom of 1887, a real estate company encouraged a group of Congregationalists in and around Claremont to establish a college which presently was named Pomona. The founding fathers in one of their first meetings passed resolutions that "the founding of a college of the New England type in Southern California is desirable" [35] and that precisely is what they produced.

The rapid influx of population, the extraordinary number of educated and literary persons included among the immigrants, and the immense wealth released by the gold mines all combined to accelerate the development of civilization on the California frontier. No other region at any period in the nation's history saw such a fantastic growth. In a brilliant book, *San Francisco's Literary Frontier*, Franklin Walker has described the rapidity with which the Pacific Coast acquired sophistication. "The interest of San Franciscans in reading prompted the establishment in the mid-fifties of three public libraries—the Mercantile Library, the Mechanics' Institute Library, and the Odd Fellows' Library," Professor Walker writes. Various societies, including the California Academy of Science, were organized in the early days. "The capital of the West supported in abundance journals through which its writers could get their training and reach their public," he continues. "As early as 1850 there were fifty printers working at their trade in the fast-growing city. San Francisco boasted that in the mid-fifties it published more newspapers than London, that in its first decade it published more books than did all the rest of the United States west of the Mississippi. Whatever voice the Western frontier might develop was sure of expression in its many literary organs, among which the *Pioneer,* the *Golden Era,* the *Hesperian,* the *Californian,* and the *Overland Monthly* could compare with the best Eastern journals." [36] It looked as if the blight which afflicts literary periodicals in this country had been arrested in the bright sunshine of California, but unhappily only two or three of the journals which began so brilliantly survived for long.

The professions and backgrounds of the two editors of the *Californian,* the first newspaper, published in Monterey in 1846, typify the kind of men who brought their talents to the new country. One was Walter Colton, a preacher and former editor of a paper in Philadelphia. The other was Robert Semple, a Kentuckian who practiced dentistry, medicine, and printing, and was a political agitator. The next paper was the *California Star,* published in San Francisco by Sam Brannan, the Mormon elder. The two papers united to form the first successful daily newspaper in the West under a new name, the *Alta Californian.* "By the time the Alta celebrated its fifth birthday," says Walker, "there were twelve other dailies in the city, and several times that number of weeklies; nearly every small town in the state also had a local journal. . . . Bancroft estimated that over a thousand men were occupied in journalism during the fifties, and that Californians supported more newspapers per man than any other people in the country." [37]

Though the quality of the papers varied widely, they provided reading matter and enlightenment for thousands. When editors were too busy or too lazy to compose original matter, they clipped material from Eastern papers and magazines, or simply reprinted excerpts from English books. They also accepted local contributions. During heated political campaigns, editors and patrons alike took pens in hand to express their opinions, frequently in heavy-handed satires, both prose and verse. On the California frontier there was no lack of journalistic reading matter or opportunity for self-expression.

The most successful and longest-lived literary periodical was the *Golden Era,* established in San Francisco in 1852. It was a weekly which lasted for forty-one years and was a training school for Bret Harte and many another Western writer. The *Era* encouraged originality, to be sure, but like the newspapers it aided in popularizing English writers. Such contributions cost nothing more than a few minutes' labor with scissors and paste. For example, the *Era* ran serially Dickens' *Bleak House* and many other uncopyrighted works by

English and Continental authors, past as well as contemporary.[38] Because of diligent promotion by the *Era's* business managers, every mining camp and country town had copies of this journal, which was both lively and eclectic. Its influence in fostering an interest in literature and familiarizing the frontier public with amusing as well as informative reading matter is incalculable.

No other frontier ever had so many writers. California then as now was a land of dramatic contrasts. It has always cried out for description, analysis, adulation, or damnation. A newcomer with even the faintest literary impulse and the slenderest ability heard the Muses calling. Articles, poems, pamphlets, and books poured from presses always ready to lend a hand to a willing author whether he wrote hoax or history. Professor Franklin Walker required a precise four hundred pages, succinct and closely written, to chronicle the extraordinary literary output of San Francisco between the years 1848 and 1875. Many of these writers were women, a great swarm of whom contributed to the *Golden Era* and other periodicals. One poetess writing under the unlikely name of Minnie Myrtle attracted the attention of Joaquin Miller and became his wife. Minnie had fallen under the spell of Byron and did her best to imitate him. Indeed, most of them sought to imitate the romantic English poets, English novelists, or genteel essayists. If they could have reproduced the literary atmosphere of London or Edinburgh as they understood it, they would have imported it whole to San Francisco.

Some of the most original of the California writers, Joaquin Miller, Ambrose Bierce, and Bret Harte drank deep of Burns, Byron, and Scott and showed the influence of British writers. Eventually all of them went to England and became thoroughly Anglophile. It is true that they capitalized on their "westernness" in England. Miller even wore western garb in English drawing rooms, whooped and hollered at social gatherings, and on at least one occasion crawled across the floor and bit a lady's leg to prove his untamed western quality. But they all wanted to be accepted as writers in the English tradition. If English critics had not rebelled at Miller's imitativeness, he would have been happy to regard England as his spiritual home. Bret Harte was so indoctrinated with England that he decided to spend the rest of his life there. Another California writer, Charles Stoddard, who had lived for a time in London with Miller, dedicated himself to the English tradition and reached the acme of literary bliss when he went to Stratford and received permission to sleep in Anne Hathaway's bed.[39] A final summation of these writers' notions of their indebtedness to England came from the pen of Bierce: "For nearly all that is good in our American civilization we are indebted to England; the errors and mischiefs are of our own creation. In learning and letters, in art and science of government, America is but a faint and stammering echo of England. The English are undoubtedly our intellectual superiors." [40] This from one of the most "western" and American of writers! Of all the significant authors who found inspiration on the California frontier, Mark Twain was the one who showed the least willingness to bow to English tradition. And even he took almost childish pleasure in the doctoral gown with which Oxford recognized his genius.

From the earliest days, the theatre had an important place in California as if it anticipated the time when a type of dramatic entertainment would become one of California's principal industries. Furthermore, upon no other frontier did the theatre come into full flower so rapidly and exert so great a social influence. The presence of many sophisticated people with a taste for drama and the wealth to support the theatre makes the phenomenal theatrical history of the region understandable. Dramatic companies swarmed to California; some of the stars of the period in the East and in Europe heard about California and headed for the gold fields. Even before gold was discovered theatrical entertainment had begun at San Francisco in a place known as "Jim Smith's Dramatic Adobe." [41] On April 19, 1848, the *Californian* carried a notice of the organization of an amateur theatrical club at Sonoma; by the autumn of 1849 Sacramento was boasting a fully-equipped theatre; and in the following January San Francisco celebrated the opening of Washington Hall, a theatre over Foley's Saloon.[42] From then onward, theatres and play performances multiplied.

An extraordinary characteristic of the dramatic entertainment offered in the early days was its high quality. Shakespeare, for example, was one of the most popular playwrights. During the first decade Californians had an opportunity of seeing twenty-two separate plays by Shakespeare,[43] a record which New York could hardly equal. The favorite play was *Richard III*, with *Hamlet, Othello, Macbeth, Romeo and Juliet* and *The Merchant of Venice* not far behind. Other English classics were popular. Massinger's *New Way to Pay Old Debts*, Otway's *Venice Preserved*, and the plays of Goldsmith and Sheridan delighted audiences in San Francisco and other frontier towns. In addition, the theatres offered favorites from the contemporary London stage, especially the plays of Bulwer-Lytton and George Colman the Younger, the usual farces and afterpieces, and a little later Italian opera and other musical attractions. When the temperance movement hit California in the 'fifties, the theatres did their part, especially with one play entitled *The Drunkard; or, The Fallen Saved*, described as "a beautiful Moral Drama." [44]

The best historian of the California theatre in this period, Professor George R. MacMinn, makes a shrewd observation on the vogue of Shakespeare as evidence of the desire to reproduce the cultivation of the past: "From a psychological point of view it seems sure that the very vanity of the San Franciscans would demand that they have their Shakespeare and have him abundantly. Easterners, as soon as they became transmuted into Westerners, as soon as they decided to stay and join in building the new Athens as well as the new Tyre of the Pacific, renounced the old complacency of Boston, New York, Philadelphia, and rapidly developed the super complacency of San Francisco. The achievement of law and order, even the acquisition of wealth, absorbed their ambition no more than did the possession and advancement of culture." [45] And MacMinn quotes Hubert Howe Bancroft, California historian contemporary with the events, on the "improving" quality of the theatre, at the same time warning that Bancroft may have exaggerated a mite. "The effect of the drama on California was most beneficial," Bancroft wrote. ". . . When theatrical performances of the better sort were offered there was a marked decline in the patronage of the gaming-table and liquor saloons. . . . As amusements of a higher order were introduced, those of the baser sort lost their charm. . . . Far above the average theatre-goer of New York, London, and Paris, in refined taste and appreciation were those of San Francisco." [46] Already the complacency of San Francisco was evident, but undoubtedly the theatre with its repertory of the best English drama made an important contribution to the civilization of the new country.

Some of the first pioneers to reach California brought enough books with them to keep alive the literary tradition. Mrs. Louise Clappe—the "Dame Shirley" of the famous *Letters*—describes the little library which she and her physician-husband kept in a candle box at Indian Bar in 1851. It contained "a Bible and Prayer

Book, Shakespeare, Spenser, Coleridge, Shelley, Keats, Lowell's *Fable for Critics,* Walton's *Compleat Angler,* and some Spanish books—spiritual instead of material lights, you see." [47] Mrs. Clappe, to be sure, had been brought up in the shadow of Amherst College and was therefore more learned than most, but other early Californians brought along similar libraries. Bookstores did well; book collecting as a hobby flourished from the first decade; and public libraries got an early start. This bookishness on the part of Californians would in time produce a network of public libraries the like of which few other regions could equal. By 1878 the development of libraries had reached such proportions that Mrs. Flora Haines Apponyi was moved to publish a book entitled *The Libraries of California* which required more than three hundred pages to describe the principal book collections.

Much incidental light on the culture of California appears in Mrs. Apponyi's book. For one thing she herself was not satisfied with the cultural manifestations displayed by the public. Like hundreds of other militant civilizers, she was out to do battle against materialism, vulgarity, and purse-proud ostentation. To that end she rebuked a recent boast of San Francisco describing the quantities of diamonds possessed by its women. It would be better, she warned, if Californians would take more pride in their books and their interest in art.[48] She then proceeded to point out that some Californians were connoisseurs of both books and art. For example, Charles and M. H. De Young, proprietors of the *San Francisco Chronicle*, had "at their elegant residence on Eddy Street, one of the most tastefully fitted up libraries in the city," containing about a thousand volumes of literature, "well selected, with some choice editions." The library also contained objects of art, pictures, engravings, busts, an "elegant and complicated music box," and "a beautiful transparent glass decanter, at the bottom of which is a musical contrivance . . . which . . . plays the 'Miserere' from Trovatore and the 'Mandolinita.' " [49] The late Governor Haight had a fine collection on the history of Scotland and certain paintings praised by Mrs. Apponyi, one being "a sweet-faced school girl standing before the blackboard, chalk in hand, gravely looking askance." [50] Milton S. Latham filled his San Francisco library with fine works of English history and literature, and varied objects of art including busts of Shakespeare, Milton, Washington, and Webster. His chief treasure was Hiram Powers' life-size nude representing California, a female in "spotless marble . . . the noble face bent slightly forward with a far-seeing look; pride, courage, resolution in her countenance as if reading her glorious future." [51]

The libraries described by Mrs. Apponyi were filled with English classics. Many Elizabethan books appear in the lists which include Hakluyt, Shakespeare, Spenser, and most of the great writers of the sixteenth century, as well as later English authors. Some of these books, she states, had been brought to California by the pioneers. When J. S. Hittell wrote his *Resources of*

California in 1874 he could claim that the "public libraries of the State in addition to those belonging to the schools number thirty, with 300,000 volumes, including the Mercantile of 30,000, Mechanics' of 20,000, and the Odd Fellows of 18,000, in San Francisco." [52] Californians were not going to be cut off from their inherited tradition of literature.

One of the most amazing booksellers and collectors was Hubert Howe Bancroft, a Yankee via the Ohio frontier, who reduced research to an efficient production line and made an industry of writing history. Beginning in 1859, he brought together the best historical library in the West, hired a stable of research workers and writers, and by 1891, completed thirty-nine volumes on the history of the West. He also published in 1890 an incredible book entitled *Literary Industries* in which he described his methods and gave himself credit for being the bringer of light to the Pacific Coast. In a literary way, he is a fitting contemporary of Collis Huntington, Leland Stanford, and other cold-blooded captains of industry. His accomplishments were great;[53] he salvaged a vast amount of the raw material of history; he and his hireling writers made the history available; and in time he sold his magnificent collection to the University of California. Whatever one may think of his methods, Bancroft with his books did much to turn Westerners' attention to their own backgrounds and to give them a sense of being a part of an historical pageant. An active promoter, he saw to it that his histories reached the widest possible audience.

By the end of the third decade after the gold rush, the older settled areas of California had developed a complex society made up of many conflicting elements. The intellectual and spiritual metropolis was, of course, San Francisco. Far to the South, Los Angeles was still a country town living on hope and hot air while it advertised its climate, orange groves, and sub-divisions. As each new area attracted inhabitants, it underwent the now familiar process which transfigured a wilderness into conventional community life. California saw a succession of frontiers grow into urban societies. What made California's frontiers different from all others was the speed with which changes occurred. Culture no less than cauliflowers grew faster in the sunshine under irrigation. Every new community, crude and crass as it might be, had its vigorous cultural custodians fighting for the souls and minds of men. Sometimes they won a victory when they least expected it. For example, frenetic real estate booms in Southern California left an inevitable trail of bankrupt hotels, and more than one college had its beginning in a defunct hotel which real estate promoters were glad to unload at a bargain.

The economic opportunities of California brought immense wealth to men who had little concern for anything else. Their wealth brought power, and with power came pride of purse and an arrogance characteristic of the parvenu. Men worshipped the golden calf unashamed. Material prosperity in the eyes of many a Californian was the chief end of man. John S. Hittell, a talented journalist who had tramped across the plains to California in 1849, made himself the laureate of California's material progress. He became almost lyrical when he considered it. "If I were a poet and felt myself capable of maintaining the epic flight," he wrote in the preface to *The Resources of California,* "I think I could find in the great Californian gold discovery and its results a subject more congenial to the taste of this age, richer in impressive suggestions, in strange and romantic incidents, and generally in material for a great poem, than the conquest of Troy or Jerusalem, the adventures of Ulysses or Aeneas." Then Hittell sat down and wrote *A Brief History of Culture* (1875) to prove that "the useful arts have made the chief epochs of history and are the main bases of civilization." The world had come to a great fulfillment in his time, and the most glorious of all periods was the "Age of Steam," Hittell believed. "The superiority of our time over antiquity is due . . . to the possession of machinery," he exulted as he proclaimed "James Watt, next to Gutenberg, the greatest modern benefactor of our race." [54]

Yet the same society that produced Hittel also stirred Josiah Royce's imagination and made him an idealistic philosopher. He too analyzed California's development and wrote a history of the frontier period which bore as a subtitle, "A Study of American Character." And he declared on the last page of this history that he had come to see in California's annals "a process of divinely moral significance." [55] Hittell glorified the steam engine; Royce's first essay, as Franklin Walker points out, was "a plea for poetry as man's greatest spiritual food." [56] Both had received inspiration from the seething and varied life on the Pacific coast.

The power of materialistic influences in California served to intensify the efforts of the apostles of enlightenment. Their converts included philanthropists who poured out their wealth to establish cultural and educational institutions. Hundreds of examples might be cited but few benefactions so dramatically illustrate their success as does the Henry E. Huntington Library and Art Gallery at San Marino. Collis Huntington, one of the builders of the Central Pacific Railway, ridiculed his colleague, Leland Stanford, for giving his fortune to found a university and referred to it as "Stanford's circus." But when his nephew Henry, who had inherited part of his uncle's fortune, was trying to decide what to do with his money, he was persuaded to found a great research library and art gallery. A wise scientist and humanistic scholar, Dr. George Ellery Hale, director of Mt. Wilson Observatory, was Huntington's closest confidant in the critical years when he was planning his institution. Hale believed that the most important contribution which Huntington could make would be to found an institution which would foster the study of Anglo-American civilization. The idea appealed to Huntington who himself had notions of the glories of the English background. Had he not spent millions already in acquiring English books and manuscripts from which the story of our common heritage could be written? He also collected English portraits of the eighteenth century. It is said that those faultlessly dressed men and women painted by Reynolds, Gainsborough, Lawrence, and Romney pleased Huntington because he thought they represented the "solid" qualities of English tradition. At any rate he gave his vast collections and millions in endowment to further the study of a civilization sufficiently vigorous to assimilate even the indigestible elements which had poured into California. The Huntington Library and its research program are proof of the powerful influence of English culture on California's last frontier.

Instruments of Civilization:
Spiritual Agencies

OF ALL the agencies utilized by man in maintaining traditional civilization on the successive frontiers in America, it should now be abundantly clear that none was more effective than organized religion. Some historians may argue that the frontier was the last place where traditionalism might be expected to prevail, especially in the sphere of religion; that the frontier did strange things to religion; that it altered and reshaped religious customs, practices, and even creeds; that new and original beliefs developed in America where the lack of restrictions and the freedom of the frontier zones gave license for the expression of individuality in religion as in everything else.[1] But that is only a half-truth which ignores the long development of religion from the days of Luther and Calvin onward, especially the development of religion in Great Britain whence came the influences which dominated the principal frontier zones except the Spanish Southwest and a few scattered areas elsewhere.

The types of religion which exerted the greatest influences on the frontiers from Jamestown to San Francisco were outgrowths of the faiths which had stirred the British Isles in the sixteenth and seventeenth centuries. English and Scottish Protestantism possessed a dynamic energy which not even the great expanses of the New World could dissipate. Even the older faith of Rome which also made its impact upon the English colonies and retained a vitality throughout the period of westward expansion was initially English Catholicism. In the Southwest, Spanish Catholicism, of course, gave its characteristic qualities to the civilization of that region. In California before the American occupation Spanish Jesuits and Franciscans were responsible for a paternalistic mission life, but after the Americans came, Protestant hordes swept over the missions leaving little except a colorful and poetic legend. The Catholics who came in the post-gold-rush days were of varied origins—French, German, English—but not predominantly Spanish. In the Mid-West, French Catholics were first in the field, but they too were overwhelmed in numbers by Protestants. Only in Louisiana was there an appreciable enclave of French Catholicism that left a permanent impression. The most important non-English Catholic influences appeared after the periods that we have been discussing, with the advent of large numbers of Irish, German, Polish, Italian, and other Continental Catholics. The early frontier societies that were most characteristic of the westward expansion were prevailingly Protestant, and of the Protestants the dissenting groups displayed the greatest energy.

The first settlers in Virginia brought with them the concept of the Anglican establishment, of a state church, and they could not conceive of society without formal religion as a part of life. Much has been written about the negligence of religion in colonial Virginia and the low state of the clergy, but actually religion played an important part in the establishment of English culture in the Chesapeake Bay region. Physical terrain and wilderness conditions altered certain customs. For example, many planters lived too far away to bury their dead in churchyards and had to be content with family burying grounds. Country churches could not boast vested choirs and the kind of ritual customary in cities. Robert Carter of Corotoman, one of the wealthiest planters in colonial Virginia, probably expressed the point of view of the majority of Anglicans in the colonies when he wrote to his agent in London concerning the religious education of his sons: "Let others take what courses they please in the bringing up of their posterity, I resolve the principles of our holy religion shall be instilled into mine betimes; as I am of the Church of England way, so I desire they should be. But the high-flown up top notions and the great stress that is laid upon ceremonies, any further than decency and conformity, are what I cannot come into the reason of. Practical godliness is the substance— these are but the shell." [2] Carter was one of the most worldly of men, but like William Byrd of Westover and most of his class, he believed that the Established Church, modified in its externals by new conditions, was essential to the civilization which they wanted to perpetuate. Throughout the Southern colonies, the Anglican Church was a bulwark of spiritual as well as political conservatism. But the Episcopal Church was not an important factor in westward expansion after the Revolution, partly because it was tainted in the minds of many patriots with an affiliation with the late enemy, partly because it was considered the religion of aristocrats, and partly because it lacked the missionary zeal to reach the plain people who made up the majority of the emigrants to the West.

The reverse was true of the Dissenting faiths. Puritanism in its various manifestations in New England had been a way of life, a part of the everyday existence of men, and not something put on on Sunday. New England towns in the earlier days had often grown by congregations splitting off and migrating with their ministers to new sites. The strict moral code of the Puritans implied an active concern of the churches for the behavior and welfare of their members and indeed for the whole community, whether within the bosom of the church or outside. And the welfare of the community also implied a concern for education which became a characteristic of New Englanders wherever they went.

Few of the Dissenting sects exceeded the Presbyterians in evangelical zeal during the late years of the eighteenth century and the first half of the nineteenth. Presbyterianism was the religion of the Scotch-Irish frontiersmen who pushed westward from Pennsylvania and from the highlands of Virginia and the Carolinas. They were among the hardiest of the pioneers, and the religious leaders were men of learning, many of whom had degrees from Scottish universities. They were as convinced of the civilizing value of Greek and Latin as they were of the truth of Holy Writ and when they combined the classics and the Bible in their educational efforts, they were certain that they had found the way to cultural and spiritual salvation. After the Act of Union in 1801 which brought Congregationalists and Presbyterians together as joint agents in the missionary enterprise in the West, their influence was even greater. The Congregationalists feared that their form of church polity, suited though it was to the compact towns of New England, would not provide an effective organization for the sparsely settled regions of the West. Since the Congregationalists of western Massachusetts and Connecticut retained a greater degree of doctrinal conservatism than the more liberal churches in the urban areas in the East, it was easy for them to affiliate with the Presbyterians who were equally conservative in matters of doctrine. Their alliance for the spiritual conquest of the West proved an excellent arrangement, though some Congregationalists declared that the Presbyterians swallowed them up. "Congregationalism," observes an historian of American home missions, "was likened to a river which took its origin in New England and flowed into a Presbyterian ocean in the West." [3] Presbyterian or Congregationalist as they might be, hundreds of devoted preachers carried the light of religion and learning to raw communities throughout the West.

Beginning in 1797 with a revival conducted in Logan County, Kentucky, by James McGready, a Presbyterian preacher, a wave of religious excitement swept the West for the next decade. This period, called the Second Awakening by analogy with the Great Awakening in the eighteenth century, or sometimes the Great Revival, was marked by the development of the camp meeting as a means of reaching the great masses of the people. These meetings, providing drama, excitement, and social contacts to a people living isolated in scattered settlements, attracted everybody, good and bad. Under the lash of clerical oratory, congregations sometimes broke into wild hysteria, but the excesses have been greatly exaggerated by sensational writers. Camp meetings could also be as solemn and decorous as a service in a New England meeting house.[4] Started by the Presbyterians, they became a characteristic feature of Methodist revivalism in the West, though they were never officially recognized by the Methodist church conferences. Nevertheless they helped to win thousands of converts to Methodism which by the second decade of the nineteenth century had overtaken Presbyterianism as the most dynamic of the frontier faiths.

Much nonsense has been written about the emotionalism of the Methodist preachers. The Methodists, as their name suggests, believed in an orderly system of worship, and many of their leaders, including Bishop Francis Asbury, frowned on too much "enthusiasm" or emotionalism. Like the Jesuits, they had a system almost military in its organization which suited conditions of Western society. Circuit riders received appointments from the bishop of the church conference having jurisdiction over a particular territory, and these itinerant preachers, riding through the wilderness, carried the gospel to the most distant settlements. At first the Methodists did not try to build churches but preached in homes, barns, or the open fields wherever they could gather a congregation. In their saddlebags they also carried books, pamphlets, and magazines which often constituted the only reading matter that ever reached many pioneers. Though not every preacher lived up to the high ideals of John Wesley, prevailingly the Methodist preachers were a self-sacrificing and devoted group who did much to civilize the West. The integrity, courage, and common sense of circuit riders like Peter Cartwright won respect wherever they went. The hardihood of the circuit riders gave currency to a saying when the weather was too bitterly cold for most mortals to stir abroad that "there is nothing out today but crows and Methodist preachers." [5]

The civilizing influence of the itinerant Methodist preacher and the literature that he distributed is incalculable, but it is a subject that deserves further investigation. Certainly he did much to bring a notion of learning and letters to people whom not even the Presbyterians could reach. John Wesley, the founder of Methodism, had edited a sort of "Great Books" series called the "Christian Library" in fifty volumes for the instruction of the faithful; and he had insisted upon his preachers reading.[6] Self-education through reading became a definite part of Methodist teaching. When the Methodists had transferred their evangelical zeal to the Western frontier, they were still concerned with edification as well as salvation. "Frontier Methodism," remarks one historian, "was far more solidly based than is usually pictured. It was by no means all froth. The long lists of books, Bibles, hymn books, Disciplines, and church periodicals sold to the people by the circuit riders, all of whom were agents for the Methodist Book Concern, are evidence that the amount of religious instruction afforded the people of the frontier was not inconsiderable." [7] The circuit rider as book agent, as a carrier of letters and learning, even on the modest level that his own background and the capacity of his saddlebags could provide, is a theme worthy of our respect— and our study. The dissemination of books in the West became a particular preoccupation of the Methodists. The General Conference of 1800 declared that "it shall be the duty of every preacher who has charge of a circuit to see that his circuit is supplied with books" and two investigators for the Massachusetts Missionary Society reported after a trip through the West in 1814 that the activity of the Methodists in distributing books "puts to blush all other charitable institutions in the United States." [8]

Like the Methodists, the Baptists made an enormous appeal to the populations who moved westward in the early nineteenth century. They had increased from about ten thousand in the whole American colonies at the beginning of the Revolution to approximately one hundred thousand in 1800, and they continued to gain rapidly after the Great Revival.[9] Unlike the Methodists and the Presbyterians, they had no centralized church organization to direct mission enterprises, but their very lack of a hierarchic organization, combined with the simplicity of Baptist doctrines, made it easy to form churches wherever a handful of Baptists found themselves. They had to ask authority of no one save God and their consciences. They might also depend for their services upon a local preacher who farmed on weekdays and preached on Sundays. Less concerned about a learned ministry than any of the other sects, they placed their trust in zeal—and they multiplied amazingly.

Out of the turmoil incidental to the Great Revival came a number of schisms among the evangelical denominations active in the West. Doctrinally conservative, the Presbyterians were quick to scent heresy and to throw out the unorthodox. As a result, they soon began to divide by fission. New Lights, Cumberland Presbyterians, Seceders, Old School and New School Presbyterians, and many other names for dissident groups indicate the division within the ranks. The Baptists and Methodists were also riven by controversy. But these sectarian divisions owe less to the frontier than they do to the beliefs implicit in Protestantism. They merely illustrate a tendency which had been in operation since the Reformation. When the Reformers conceded that men could read and interpret the Scriptures according to the dictates of their consciences and could dispense with a priest as intercessor with God, they opened a Pandora's box which they could never close thereafter. The religious fractionalization in the early nineteenth century, especially in the Western zones, was a continuation of a process which had been particularly active in seventeenth-century England. Frontier conditions favored but did not necessarily originate schism. If a London clergyman of 1645 had found himself at a meeting of some of the controversial church gatherings in Kentucky in 1810, let us say, he would have felt completely at home. The sectarian tradition of British Protestantism with its ability to develop new life by cellular fission carried on throughout the expansion westward and reached its ultimate development in Los Angeles County in our time. Yet there is no evidence that this fission resulted in loss of energy.

Sectarian competition, indeed, helped to generate activity and spur religious groups to extraordinary efforts in establishing churches and schools. Nearly all of the frontier colleges which sprang up like mushrooms in the nineteenth century were religious in origin. Each denomination felt that it must have a college if it expected to keep pace with its rivals. Even the Baptists joined in the educational race. "Nearly all our colleges are . . . the creations of the different religious denominations which divide our poeple," declared President F. A. P. Barnard of the University of Mississippi in 1856. "They are regarded as important instrumentalities, through which the peculiarities of doctrine which distinguish its founders are to be maintained, propagated, or defended. It is this which has led to the great multiplication of collegiate institutions in our country, and which is daily adding to their number." [10] The multiplication of colleges did not receive unalloyed praise from all observers. Concerning the crop of colleges which germinated in Illinois in the 1830's, one commentator remarked that "a settler could hardly encamp on the prairies but a college would spring up beside his wagon." [11] These institutions, often colleges in name only, with a clergyman and his wife composing the academic staff, obviously sought to emphasize the dogmas of their sects, but they also provided a surprising amount of cultural training. Many an intellectual leader in the West owed his education to some college which flourished a few years and died.

Jealousies and suspicions among the rival sects resulted in the constant multiplication of colleges. In Indiana, Southerners feared Northern Congregationalism as exemplified in the activities of Yale missionaries who sometimes aroused hostility by their Yankee orthodoxy. So strongly was college education identified with Northerners in some minds that one observer reported that certain Indiana communities were prejudiced against "colleges, pianos and Yankees." [12] Because the Methodists of Indiana were so upset over the domination of Indiana University by Presbyterians, they organized in 1837 Indiana-Asbury College, later DePauw University. Not only rivalry among the sects but the haunting fear of Roman Catholicism drove the Protestants to found schools and colleges as a bulwark against the Catholic tide which they believed would sweep West with increased immigration from Europe. In a tractate entitled *A Plea for the West,* published at Cincinnati in 1836, Lyman Beecher stressed the danger and urged the founding of "literary and moral" institutions which would influence the public by producing teachers and preachers to battle on their home fronts.

Of colleges which have survived, at least 182 were founded before the Civil War,[13] and many of these were religious institutions established in the western frontier zones. By 1830 the church movement to found colleges was in full swing and the great depression of 1837 caused only a temporary setback. Eastern religious groups felt a missionary urge to help the emigrants to the West by sending them teachers and preachers. Because of the great prestige of Princeton and Yale among orthodox Presbyterians and Congregationalists respectively, it is estimated that twenty-five colleges owed their foundation to Princeton's influence and sixteen to Yale's.[14]

The West soon learned that sustenance for its scores of struggling colleges must come from churches in the East, and academic beggars in the guise of "agents," preachers, and presidents swarmed like locusts out of the West. We might point out parenthetically that conditions are now reversed. No shrewd college president in the East nowadays feels that he has done his duty unless he has "approached" the oil-rich millionaires of California and Texas. So insistent were the demands from the West that religious groups organized associations of various kinds to bring some method into their Western philanthropies—and weed out the fraudulent claims. The most famous of these organizations was the Society for the Promotion of Collegiate and Theological Education in the West, founded in New York on June 30, 1843. It survived for more than a quarter of a century and its records provide a significant insight into the religious influences upon education in the period of expansion.

Conservative Easterners sometimes expressed fears that Western colleges were radical and given to teaching doctrines dangerous to church and commonwealth. One of the concerns of the begging agents was to disabuse prospective philanthropists of such ideas and to prove that Western colleges were both pious and devoted to the ideals of business and trade. "The learning, religion, and the living ministry bestowed on the great West by these colleges unite in special benefit to mercantile morality and hence to the safety and value of business engagements there formed," one speaker declared before the Society for the Promotion of Collegiate and Theological Education in the West. "Eastern merchants have an especial and increasing concern in the commerical integrity of this immense market for Eastern industry. However lightly men think of religion and of culture attending it, they are 'terribly in earnest' as to the counterfeits and cheats which irreligion and ungodliness impose on them. They forget that, like the pillars of Hercules, Education and Religion define and defend the path of trade . . . These colleges thus plead to every enlightened merchant his own self-preservation, and the perpetuity of the commercial virtues which adorn his own profession." [15] The identity of godliness, education, and commercial prosperity should not be considered an indication of hypocrisy on the part of nineteenth-century preachers and educators. This doctrine was a fundamental tenet of middle-class culture and comes down directly from the English tradition of the sixteenth and seventeenth centuries. [16]

Far from being radical, the Western colleges founded by religious groups were more conservative ideologically than many of the older Eastern institutions. Socially the Western college might be democratic; it might open its doors to women on an equal footing with men; it might not condone the snobbery of exclusive clubs and fraternities; but ideologically, Western colleges were rarely given to experimentation or speculative thinking. Even today in the West boards of trustees worry about radicalism in a way that seems ridiculous to many of their counterparts in the East. The typical frontier college wanted to reproduce both the religion and the culture which their founders had regarded as orthodox, and most of these colleges were determined to have no traffic with uncertified notions and beliefs.

Although the Protestant tendency to sectarianism made for divisiveness as between denominations, such rivalries helped to solidify congregations within themselves. In the face of outside competition they worked all the harder to unify themselves and to bring the individual members of the congregation into a cohesive group.

Aside from the strictly religious function of frontier churches, they performed an equally important service by providing focal centers for cultural activities in their respective communities. During the seventeenth and eighteenth centuries, the church was usually the first structure erected after the settlers had built a stockade and living quarters. The church would be used on weekdays as a school until some other provision could be made, or as a hall for any appropriate public gathering. Later, in the nineteenth century, the schoolhouse was usually the earliest public building, and there religious services would be held on Sundays until the various denominations could erect churches of their own.[17] This shift in priority from church to school may indicate the growing concept of education as a way to social salvation, a gospel which gained momentum throughout the nineteenth century. Be that as it may, churches and schools were closely linked throughout the period of expansion, and in addition to serving as guardians of morals and religion, the churches acted as a centrifugal force in society. An attachment to some church, even when the bonds of piety had weakened, held families to a definite social organization which kept them from drifting into individual isolation or social anarchy.

The country church was often the only instrumentality of communal activity, or indeed of social communication between families scattered over a wide area. On Sundays, farmers and their families put on their best clothes, rode or drove in wagons or buggies to the nearest church of their persuasion, and spent most of the day in spiritual and social recreation. At some country churches, when the weather was favorable, the preacher might provide a sermon in the morning, adjourn for "dinner on the grounds," and give his congregation another sermon in the afternoon, or perhaps a song service might take the place of the second sermon. But long before the service, the congregation had gathered in the churchyard for talk. They exchanged information about weather, crops, prices, and politics. Though it was generally considered improper and irreligious to transact business on Sunday at church, arrangements were made for completing many a trade at a more appropriate occasion later. Young people regarded church as a legitimate place for courting, modestly of course, according to a fairly rigid decorum. There they made their dates for future meetings, for parties and social gatherings. The church picnic was the occasion for friendly competition between housewives when the relative merits of potato versus blackberry pie might become more important for the moment than questions concerning infant damnation or salvation by grace.

The "protracted meetings," as late summer revivals were called, brought congregations together after the rush of farm work was over for a week or more of religious services. The regular preacher was usually assisted by a visiting minister who brought new ideas and a fresh personality to the community. The more prosperous members of the congregation would compete for the privilege of entertaining in turn the preachers, who always brought news of the greater world beyond their parishioners' normal horizons. These protracted meetings served a purpose far beyond mere religious refreshment; they were social festivals which brought together people who spent much of their time working in isolation on their widely separated farms. Attendance at the protracted meetings was not limited to the members of the particular church. Presbyterians and Baptists, for example, might turn out for a Methodist service and take an active part. Such gatherings frequently helped to break down denominational barriers and to knit communities together, though it must be added that a tactless or narrow-minded preacher who stressed his own theological dogma too rigidly occasionally plunged a community into religious controversy. In any case, the services stimulated discussion and social activity which broke the monotony and relieved the barrenness of country life.

Destitute of colorful ritual, the Protestant churches on the frontier made few contributions to the esthetic development of their members, but in the realm of music the churches offered an opportunity for the active participation of everyone in an esthetic experience, limited though it might be. The denominations varied in their attitude toward music in the church. The Presbyterians and Congregationalists clung to the tradition of Psalm-singing, though the prejudice against the singing of hymns and the use of musical instruments gradually relaxed during the nineteenth century. The strongest objections to music in the church service came from the most conservative wing of the Presbyterians, the Associated Reformed branch known colloquially as "Seceders." They insisted upon the restriction of singing to the metrical versions of the Psalms inherited from the seventeenth century; they violently opposed the free renditions in Isaac Watts' *Psalms of David,* first published in 1715, and of course they would have nothing to do with Watts' *Hymns* (1709). But no inhibitions about music curbed the Methodists and Baptists. They made the most of hymn-singing as a part of their worship, and their congregational singing during regular services and at revivals provided a great emotional release. Watts' hymns were widely used and became a part of the emotional and esthetic experience of thousands of men and women in the West who had few other outlets for their musical urge. Under the mystical influence of such hymns as "O God, our help in ages past," and "When I survey the wondrous cross," weary pioneers might forget the dark gloom of the forests or the dreary monotony of the prairies as they caught for a moment the vision of heavenly glory.

The Methodists laid a tremendous emphasis on hymn-singing, and for their use John and Charles Wesley wrote and published hymns which have been sung from that day to this. Charles Wesley's "Hark! the herald angels sing" and "Jesus, Lover of my soul" were part of the musical repertory not only of Methodists but of many other Protestants. The Methodist Church exercised careful supervision over its official hymnals and tried to discourage the use of song books which it did not approve. But a variety of non-canonical hymn books got into circulation, especially in the West. Some of the more popular of these books were Stith Mead's *Hymns and Spiritual Songs,* first published at Richmond, Va., in 1805, Thomas S. Hinde's *The Pilgrim Songster* (Cincinnati, 1810), and Orange Scott's *The New and Improved Camp Meeting Hymn Book* (Brookfield, Mass., 1830).[18] Like the Wesleys before them, these later song writers set religious sentiments to popular tunes which could be easily learned and remembered.

Not all of the catchy hymns pleased the preachers and stricter church folk, who felt that some of them were too "worldly," but they continued to be sung in church and out of it. Religious songs became a part of everybody's repertory and might be heard wherever people got together for a social evening. Even today many a bibulous party has been known to end singing hymns. Singing teachers drifted from community to community organizing classes. These itinerant teachers were sometimes more noted for their consumption of hard liquor than for their skill in music; their approach might be altogether secular; but their repertory was usually religious. The people liked hymn-singing and the teachers aimed at making them more proficient. Some of the religious music represented survivals from the sixteenth and seventeenth centuries, and some of it still survives in backwoods areas.[19] The folklorists have now taken notice of it and it will be embalmed for the future in monographs, in books, and on tape recorders.

The interest of frontier folk in singing may be indicated by the number of song books sold in Western stores. Advertisements of merchants frequently mention musical books of various sorts, but almost invariably they were collections of religious songs. About 1815, the first edition of *The Kentucky Harmony, or A Choice Collection of Psalm Tunes, Hymns, and Anthems . . . Well Adapted to Christian Churches, Singing Schools, or Private Societies. Selected by Ananias Davisson* was published at Harrisonburg, Virginia, and went through several editions. Many similar books followed. *The Kentucky Harmonist* (Lexington, 1817), *The Missouri Harmony* (Cincinnati, 1820), *The Columbian Harmony* (Cincinnati, 1825), *The Western Harmony* (Nashville, 1824), and dozens of other titles like these indicate the desire of authors and printers to supply song books appealing to Western interests.[20] Abraham Lincoln and Ann Rutledge are said to have learned songs from *The Missouri Harmony,* and Lincoln, like most frontiersmen, loved hymns. One of the favorite song books of the Baptists, *Conference Hymns for Social Worship,* compiled early in the nineteenth century by Dr. David Benedict, went through many editions. One hymn entitled "Prayer for the Conversion of the American Indians," must have been sung with considerable feeling by frontiersmen who stood in constant hazard of their scalps from the unconverted heathen. The hymn begins: "O'er Columbia's wide-spread forests, Haste ye heralds of the Lamb." Another hymn called "Pilgrim's Progress" emphasized the value of Bunyan's allegory.[21]

Most congregational singing in Western churches at first was without instrumental accompaniment. The fiddle was regarded as the devil's instrument suitable only for dances by the godless and not many churches could afford an organ even if they could have transported one over wilderness roads. When at last a church was able to acquire an organ, that congregation succumbed to the first of the Seven Deadly Sins, Pride. In many communities the church organ remained for years the only instrument available for serious music.

The immense importance of music to a people who might be otherwise esthetically starved was recognized by the founders of the Mormon faith. That remarkable group of pioneers who made a garden out of an intractable desert in Utah also stirred the hearts of their church members with music which they adapted from the traditional songs inherited from the past. "The music of the Mormons," one historian comments, "is a vivid reflection of the history of that extraordinary people. Hymn texts and melodies, the dance, songs of folk and individual origin, and choral and instrumental performance are forms of musical expression which record both the religious tenets and the social and political life of the Saints. Wherever he lived the Mormon and his music were inseparable companions. Thus any history of the Mormon Church is complete only if the story of its music is included." [22]

A great deal of the Mormon church music illustrates the importance which hymns had acquired in the lives of British dissenting groups since the Reformation. For many of their songs are simply adaptations of hymns which Methodists, Baptists, and other dissenting sects had made popular. The Mormons recruited many of their followers from the dissenting sects of England and Wales. So important was their missionary activity in Great Britain that they issued a newspaper there, the *Millenial Star,* first published in March, 1840, and in the same year they published an English hymnal. Many of the hymns in this volume were paraphrases of older Protestant hymns, adapted to suit the beliefs and aspirations of the Mormons. The volume was so popular that it went through nine editions in the next decade and copies were shipped to Utah for the use of the American Saints. Many English and Welsh Mormons came to Utah bringing with them their love of traditional church music. In Salt Lake City at the first celebration of "Pioneer Day" on July 24, 1849, one of the most popular numbers on the program was a song by the Welsh choir, "Wend Ye with the Saints To-day." [23]

The Mormons were the first of the Western pioneers to make use of band and stringed instrumental music in their worship. They had no inhibitions against instruments associated with the dance, for they encouraged "dancing before the Lord." Their bands included strings, wind, and percussion instruments, all of which they deemed suitable to make a joyful noise. Of all the frontier faiths, the Mormons appear to have got more fun out of their religion than any other, and one source of their pleasure was church music, much of which, however, comes straight down in the tradition of British Protestant hymnology.

One of the greatest contributions made by the Protestant evangelical groups to the intellectual and spiritual development of the isolated settlers on the Western frontiers came through their encouragement of the reading of the Bible and their practical program for providing every household with a copy of the King James Authorized Version. One of the famous hymns included in David Benedict's *Conference Hymns for Social Worship* stressed the value of the Bible. It begins:

> Holy Bible! choicest treasure,
>   Blest inheritance below,
> Purest source of pious pleasure,
>   Antidote to every woe.
>   Holy Bible!
>   Speak to men of every tongue.[24]

Fundamental in Protestant doctrine was the belief that every man, woman, and child should be able to read and appreciate the truths and beauty of the Scriptures. The early years of the nineteenth century saw the formation of many state and local Bible societies. As early as 1814 the Cincinnati Miami Bible Society was organized to distribute Bibles to the poor on the Ohio and Kentucky frontiers. Two years later, in 1816, the American Bible Society was organized in New York with all of the principal Protestant sects co-operating. Its purpose was to print and distribute Bibles throughout the world but especially in the American West where the need was great. Its goal was to place a Bible in the hands of every person capable of reading it, and within a few years its success was phenomenal.[25] The combined efforts of the Bible societies made it possible for the poorest householder to possess one book of supreme literary merit, a book furthermore which had such prestige that it possessed talismanic value. As the hymn declared, it was an "antidote to every woe," but more than that, it was a book of magnificent prose and poetry written in the simplest and purest language of the sixteenth and seventeenth centuries. The constant reading of the Bible helped to shape the language patterns of countless Americans and its rhythms were reflected in the oratory, not only of preachers, but of politicians and statesmen. The King James Version of the Bible exerted a greater influence on American imaginations and style than any other book. It is one of the literary tragedies of our age that the Bible is so little read today. Perhaps if our contemporary authors had steeped themselves more in the simple prose of the Bible, their writings would have greater precision and clarity.

When we talk of the poverty of reading matter on any of our frontiers from the seventeenth to the mid-nineteenth century, we are prone to think in quantitative terms. We are likely to forget that one book well read may have a far greater impact than dozens skimmed and tossed aside. No one can say that the Bible was not earnestly read by thousands. In pious households it was read aloud at family worship and children were accustomed from infancy to its sonorous music. Unconsciously it became a part of an esthetic experience in addition to whatever religious effect it may have had. One of the works which most influenced the style and thinking of Abraham Lincoln was the Bible. Though some of his friends described him as a free-thinker if not an infidel, others who heard him quote Scripture with respect thought him a religious man. Before he had learned to read, he had heard his mother quoting Bible verses as she worked and he had learned many of these verses by heart. "Lincoln read the Bible closely," Carl Sandburg asserts, "read it from cover to cover, was familiar with its stories and its poetry, quoted from it in his talks to juries, in political campaigns, in his speeches, and in his letters." [26] Lincoln's acquaintance with the Bible was not unusual, for the Bible was a part of the general education of every citizen. If a backwoods lawyer had to choose between Blackstone and the Bible, he was better advised to stick to citations from the Bible because jurors were more familiar with it and could be persuaded by its dramatic connotations no less than by the weight of its authority as revealed truth. In the Bible, the frontiersman had a whole library of poetry, drama, histori-cal narrative, folk tales, didactic exposition, and practically anything else his taste might require, all available in a diction and a style that have rarely been equaled in any language. The concentration upon this volume which poverty forced upon many a household was not without benefits which the modern reader might envy.

One of the aims of the Sunday-School movement which became an important factor in religious education in the early decades of the nineteenth century was to stimulate an interest in Bible-reading. Sometimes the Sunday Schools were more zealous than wise, but they at least achieved their aims of stirring up an interest in the Scriptures. Between 1805 and 1820, Sunday Schools placed a great deal of emphasis on memorizing passages from the Bible. People of all ages, from infants to grandparents, competed in contests of memory. One Sunday School reported that it had taught an old man of seventy-eight previously completely illiterate, to read the Bible with ease. Another Sunday School pupil not only recited 1,750 verses of Scripture but memorized all of Watts' Psalms and hymns, "besides fifty out of other books." [27] The memorizing of whole books of the Bible was not unusual. One girl was reported to have learned by heart everything from Genesis to Isaiah, and another all of the New Testament as well as parts of the Old.

Not only Sunday Schools but local missionary societies made the reading of the Bible one of their objectives. Frontier churches, like city churches back East, frequently had organizations of women which served a social as well as a religious purpose. In nearly every instance they emphasized the virtue of Bible reading. In 1812, when Cincinnati was still a Western outpost, women members of the Presbyterian congregation organized the Cincinnati Female Society for Charitable Purposes which met at regular intervals for "prayer and religious conversation." One third of the money it collected went to buy Bibles for distribution to the needy. The organizations intent upon providing the populace with Bibles and seeing that they read them must have been numbered by the hundreds. The value placed upon the Bible is illustrated by the rules governing the pony express riders of the firm of Russell, Majors, and Waddell, who required their riders to swear not to quarrel, use profane language, or drink intoxicating liquor. After taking this oath, the riders received a small leather-bound Bible, capable of standing rough use, which the rider was expected to carry with him. Whether these Testaments ever stopped an Indian arrow, legend does not say, but there is a perennial legend of the Testament which saves a soldier's life by stopping a bullet in time. If only for its magical value, many a man engaged in dangerous enterprises was persuaded to carry a Bible. For whatever reason, the Bible was a ubiquitous book which profoundly influenced the lives of Western settlers.

Though the Bible, of course, was the work of first importance distributed by church organizations, other pious reading matter poured out of the East to elevate and enlighten Western settlers. Eastern churches took seriously the obligation to save their Western brethren from irreligion, infidelity, and ignorance. Missionary societies by the score, local and general, sent books, tracts, magazines, and church papers to the West. In the 1820's the American Sunday School Union, a non-sectarian organization to promote religious instruction and pious reading, published *The American Sunday-School Magazine* and *The Youth's Friend* in vast numbers along with other works which were distributed throughout East and West. In 1825 the Union boasted that it had issued more than 900,000 publications in addition to its periodicals, and two years later it reported the distribution of nearly four million publications. It also distributed collections of books for Sunday School libraries. So great was the Sunday School Union's interest in the West that Francis Scott Key, author of the national anthem and a manager of the Union, in 1830 called a great meeting in Washington to discuss ways and means of extending Sunday Schools and their influence in the frontier regions of the Mississippi Valley. The prestige of the undertaking was such that Key persuaded Daniel Webster, among others, to lend his oratory to advocating this missionary enterprise.[28] Numerous other organizations, local as well as national, Eastern and also Western, published pious works for the improvement of manners and morals. The American Tract Society published millions of tracts and pamphlets which it furnished at cost to local religious societies. Each church also had its own publications including periodicals, service books, and general literature deemed appropriate. Sometimes the church presses published textbooks for use in the schools. As we have seen, the Methodists took the lead in the distribution of books. So great was its activity in the West that it incorporated in 1836 a separate branch of its publishing house as "The Western Methodist Book Concern" with headquarters in Cincinnati. In addition to the numerous periodicals published in the East, it promoted the *Pittsburgh Christian Advocate* in 1833, the *Western Christian Advocate,* first published in Cincinnati in 1834, and other later Western journals.[29] If pious literature could bring civilization to the West, the Protestant churches were determined to supply that needful commodity. The truth is that religious literature was often the only reading matter cheaply and readily available to immigrants struggling to establish themselves in frontier settlements, and it provided a basis for cultural development which we cannot afford to overlook.

The role of the churches in maintaining decorum, decency, and morality on the turbulent frontier goes without saying. One of their essential functions was to serve as moral courts and to enforce discipline in a region where the better element had to be constantly on guard against license and lawlessness. One of the problems, for instance, was to enforce some sort of restriction against drunkenness in a society where whisky could be bought for twenty-five cents a gallon and a keg of whisky with a convenient dipper was necessary to any public gathering. Even preachers sometimes took part of their pay in whisky. For example, the Reverend Joshua L. Wilson, minister of the First Presbyterian Church of Cincinnati, accepted one hundred gallons of whisky in 1807 in lieu of cash.[30] In addition to the common evil of drunkenness the churches had to combat various forms of disorder and violence, particularly sexual irregularities. All of the churches kept a sharp eye out for sin among their members and were accustomed to hail them to hearings before church courts. It is an indication of the prestige which church membership carried that expulsion from the church was regarded on the wildest frontier as a penalty to be avoided at all costs. Throughout the frontier period the churches exerted a restraining and civilizing influence which we are inclined to forget in our concentration on the lawless aspects of Western life.

Crude and lawless many Western communities were —at first. But with amazing rapidity the churches and church folk began to operate in most of these communities, and they rarely gave up until they had routed the Devil and at least some of his works. Their notions of conquering the powers of evil did not stop with victory in the realm of morality. Civilization included education, cultivation, and good manners, and the churches labored persistently on the side of the angels of cultural light. Their success was far greater than cynics have been willing to admit. The churches always fought to re-establish traditional civilization and their conservatism usually prevailed.

Instruments of Civilization: Secular Agencies

THE *New York Times Book Review* for February 22, 1953, described an ingenious craftsman who makes his living by manufacturing fake books and book-like panels to conceal liquor cabinets and wall safes. "For such orders," the *Times* reported, "he almost always recommends Sir Walter Scott. 'Almost no one,' he told us, 'is tempted to reach for a copy of *The Lady of the Lake.*' " Yet a little more than a century ago, when the Middle West was a frontier region, nobody would have dared hide anything behind *The Lady of the Lake*, or any other title by Scott, either poetry or fiction, for Scott would have been the first to attract the eye of a reader, meddlesome or otherwise. The Western frontier consumed an amazing amount of contemporary English literature, the favorite authors being Scott and Byron. When we appraise the agencies which helped to shape the minds and emotions of Americans on our successive frontiers, we must accord an important place to the persistent influence of traditional literature, especially British books read at home and in schools.

The great hold which English literature has had on

the minds of Americans has caused some academic
Cassandras to warn that we have allowed ourselves to
become unduly Anglicized, sometimes to the neglect
of any knowledge of our native literature. The current
upsurge of American nationalism has changed the
emphasis and today courses in American literature and
American civilization flourish in every college and
university. But as recently as 1944 Professor Howard
Mumford Jones of Harvard published a book lament-
ing the predominance of professional interest in English
literature to the neglect of American writers. Training in literature, he pointed out, "is education in British
literature. Not only undergraduates but our doctors of
philosophy are primarily specialists in the literature of
a foreign land. . . . The large majority of our professors
of English have only a superficial acquaintance with
American literature, and only the vaguest notion of
what scholarship under immense difficulties has accomplished in this field. . . . This is an extraordinary
state of affairs, and it is only because we are used to it
that we do not see how extraordinary it is. . . . It is
only in the United States that professors of literature
are permitted to be scandalously ignorant of their own
national achievement." [1]

As Professor Jones hastened to point out, he was not
arguing that Americans should forget their inheritance
from the literary tradition of Great Britain. He merely
wanted them to know, in addition, something about
their native literary accomplishments. The extreme emphasis on English literature in our reading habits is

not, of course, an academic phenomenon. It goes back to the beginning of our nation and continues through the nineteenth century. Only in our time have American authors taken the lead over English writers in the popular literature consumed by Americans. During most of our past history, traditional literature, first the classical heritage from Greece and Rome, and then the legacy from Britain, determined our literary culture. This literary influence manifested itself in various ways on more than one level. Literature does not necessarily connote a highbrow affectation, for literature is diverse and all of it does not require an acquaintance with recondite authors. The impact of literature may come from the daily reading of the Bible, from the stirring of the imagination by Bunyan's *Pilgrim's Progress,* or the repetition of passages from classic authors printed in McGuffey's *Eclectic Readers.* Whatever the level of literary interest and consumption, the writings of English authors profoundly affected American thinking and feeling. We have so long taken English literature for granted, like the air we breathe or the water we drink, that we forget that it has been one of the most enduring and ever-present factors in determining the contents of our minds. Whatever we are racially or whatever may be our national origins, we have turned to English literature for our main intellectual sustenance.

Writing about San Francisco in the period just after the gold rush, John S. Hittell, himself a German by extraction, described the population: "The people are mostly American by birth," he asserted, "but there are also many English, Irish, French, Germans, Italians, Spanish-Americans, Scandinavians, Dalmatians, and Chinese. There are French, German, Italian, and Spanish newspapers; French, German, and Chinese churches, and French, German, and Chinese theatrical companies." [2] Yet in spite of the polyglot population of San Francisco and California in general, Hittell declared that English was spoken with greater purity and understanding than in any other state in the Union. Newspapers in the English language, books from the pens of English authors, and even British magazines were a great force in molding the speech—and the thinking habits—of this frontier population. Hittell even takes to task Bret Harte, a popular California author, for putting into the mouths of his characters a special dialect. "Bret Harte," he says, "has attributed to the miners of California a peculiar, strongly-marked, and affected dialect, but he has drawn on his imagination for the greater part of it. A mixed population, like that in the mines, representing every state in the Union, and every county of Great Britain, could not have a dialect; and nowhere is the English language better understood, or spoken with more force, elegance, and purity by the poorer classes of people, than in this State." [3]

From the earliest times in this country, the books which immigrants brought with them exerted a greater influence on their intellectual development than we are likely to believe today when printing is so common and the means of communication so varied that we forget the impact of one or two books diligently read and re-read by our ancestors. In all of the migrations, from the settlement at Jamestown to the populating of the Western prairies, the quantity of supplies which emigrants could take along was severely limited. In the first stages, only the barest necessities could be taken, and for many years the high cost of freight prevented the transportation of nonessentials. When our ancestors carried books with them, or imported them later, they chose works which they believed would supply some essential need. We can be certain that such books were widely read and frequently served not only their owner's use but the needs of his friends and neighbors. The literary interest of a people and the influence of literature upon a population cannot be measured in quantitative terms alone. One book well-read, such as the Bible, for example, may do more to affect the style and imagination of a whole generation than the entire paperback output of the press today.

In the colonial period, the books imported and the books published on this side of the Atlantic were primarily utilitarian. Many of them of course were works of piety, for religion occupied a more significant place in American life then than now, in the Southern and Middle Atlantic colonies as well as in Puritan New England. An enormous number of the religious books read by our ancestors were devotional works and sermons intent upon instruction, not in the fine points of theology, but in a way of life. They dealt with manners, behavior, morals, and frequently with practical matters concerned with one's everyday existence. Many of them were as popular among the Anglicans of Virginia as they were among the Puritans of Massachusetts Bay. For example, Lewis Bayly's *The Practise of Pietie,* first printed about 1612, was eagerly read on both sides of the Atlantic until the nineteenth century, and in thousands of households was second only to the Bible in the readers' esteem. John Eliot thought so well of it that he translated it for the Indians. *The Practise of Pietie* was only one of many devotional books written in plain language to reach the understanding of any reader. Another popular book of this time, written from the Anglican point of view, was Richard Allestree's *The Whole Duty of Man* (1658), the very title of which indicates its scope and purpose. Such books transmitted to Americans not only the traditional Protestant ethic of England but also models of simple, direct prose which undoubtedly had an effect on the literate expression of their readers.

"How harde wyll it bee for one browghte vp amonge boockes and learned men to lyve in a barbarous place where is no learnynge and lesse cyvillytie," wrote one of John Winthrop's friends on the eve of his departure for New England.[4] The answer of Winthrop and other emigrants was to take along the books necessary to insure civility. In addition to religious works, they prized the classics, histories, legal treatises, and, of course, practical handbooks including manuals on medicine, surveying, cookery, horsemanship, and military tactics.[5] The inventories of little wilderness libraries in the seventeenth and early eighteenth centuries show a surprising distribution of the works of Homer, Plutarch, Pliny, Virgil, Seneca, Ovid, Horace, Livy, and other Greek and Roman writers. Some of these were in translation but many an emigrant brought along the originals and the necessary grammars and dictionaries to go with them. The seventeenth-century emigrants did not waste much space on contemporary belles-lettres. Copies of Shakespeare and Milton, for example, are rare in seventeenth-century book lists, but colonial readers found entertainment in the classics and even in such solid matter as sermons, which were not confined to the libraries of divines. For instance, William Byrd of Westover, certainly no paragon of piety, took almost as much pleasure in sermons as he did in his consistent reading of Greek and Latin literature. The most isolated farmhouse in the backwoods might contain the raw materials of literary learning. Civility was where one found it, and literature helped the settlers to reproduce the best of the old culture.

The books that carried the germ plasm of English civilization were many and various. Which book or books exerted the greatest influence is a matter for endless debate, but no one can deny the importance of historical and legal works in establishing among the English-speaking people of the New World a sense of continuity with the past and a feeling of respect for law which has characterized English thinking for centuries.

Richard Brathwaite in *The English Gentleman*

(1630), a book much favored in the colonies, had declared that history provides "the sweetest Recreation
of the minde," [6] and this view was merely an echo of
popular opinion. Certainly histories were second only
to religious works in popular appeal. In history and
biography, it was believed, readers would find not only
recreation but lessons of benefit in both private and
public matters. Camden's *Britannia*, Raleigh's *History
of the World*, Burnet's *History of the Reformation*,
Clarendon's *History of the Rebellion*, John Rushworth's
Historical Collections, John Foxe's *Acts and Monuments*, and dozens of other historical and biographical
works remained popular in America well into the
eighteenth century. Foxe's work, better known as the
"Book of Martyrs," must have stimulated enormously
the fear of Catholic domination and kept alive violent
Protestant prejudices, for it was widely read and the
all-too-vivid woodcuts of martyrs burning at the stake
carried a pictorial message not lost on either child or
adult.

Legal works were more generally read in the eras of
settlement than now, for nearly every literate citizen
fancied himself something of an authority on the law.
In early colonial times there was no professional group
of lawyers and every man had to be his own attorney or
depend on some neighbor more learned in such matters
than he. In Virginia, for example, planters were constantly writing to one another about legal matters, and
they collected in their libraries books which would
throw light on the tradition of law. Our ancestors

developed a great interest, not merely in cases and statutes, but in legal theory, and in theories of the state. Early libraries contained manuals such as Michael Dalton's *The Country Justice* and *The Office and Authority of Sheriffs,* and a variety of other legal works: Sir Edward Coke's *Institutes of the Laws of England* and his famous *Reports,* Sir John Fortescue's *A Learned Commendation of the Politic Laws of England,* Sir Thomas Smith's *The Commonwealth of England and Manner of Government,* and other books which discussed law and justice within the frame of the English constitution. It would be hard to overestimate the value of the self-imposed discipline in legal theory and practice which such reading gave to hundreds of citizens of the new country. Later, in the eighteenth century, Sir William Blackstone's *Commentaries on the Laws of England* (1765-69) became the bible of American lawyers. Few books in any age have had so profound an influence upon legal thought as Blackstone's *Commentaries* had upon American jurisprudence. It is estimated that more than a thousand copies of the work were shipped to the colonies before the first American edition in 1771-72.[7] In the following century, more copies of Blackstone were bought in America than in Great Britain and the *Commentaries* taught Americans the fundamental doctrines of the common law of England. Jefferson echoed the *Commentaries* in the Declaration of Independence; American writers on legal questions freely adapted matter from the *Commentaries;* and practically all lawyers in the United States before 1900 had absorbed some portion of this work. We might declare our political independence of England, but we clung to the essential core of her legal system. Backwoods lawyers with only Blackstone's *Commentaries* and a set of their own state's published statutes felt equipped to argue cases and set forth learned opinions on jurisprudence. The precedents and practices of English common law transmitted to Americans a vast body of inherited ideas concerning political rights and privileges which we have modified but never changed fundamentally.

Formal ideas on political theory came from many sources but none was more influential than the second of John Locke's *Two Treatises of Government*, first published in 1690. From this essay Jefferson took ideas reflected in the Declaration of Independence, and political thinkers for a century afterward continued to draw on Locke for inspiration, phrases, and political doctrine.[8] Country editors and prairie politicians might refer to Locke as to an oracle. If a few religious folk remembered that his *Essay Concerning Human Understanding* and *The Reasonableness of Christianity* were downright deistic in implication, many more quoted with approval the passages on natural rights in his political tracts. Works like the *Two Treatises of Government* were far-reaching and permanent in their influence.

Throughout the eighteenth and nineteenth centuries, the writings of English authors subtly molded American ideas. During the early eighteenth century,

Americans read Addison and Steele with avidity and *The Spectator* was found in countless American libraries. As the authors intended, *The Spectator* taught manners and morals while at the same time it provided entertainment. Its style was imitated by Benjamin Franklin, Washington Irving, and many a writer whose efforts never got farther than the village newspaper. Sometimes wisdom from *The Spectator* found its way into almanacs and thus into households whose owners never heard of the original London authors. In every chimney corner hung an almanac, zealously read on rainy days by frontiersmen who imbibed a little of the literary tradition from its excerpts.

Although we cannot claim that the pioneers who opened the West all carried classic English authors in their packs, Shakespeare, Milton, and Pope were so well known in frontier society that politicians quoted them with the assurance that the electorate would recognize and approve the literary allusions. Newspaper editors were fond of beginning a piece with a quotation from Shakespeare, and would-be satirists who contributed to the papers liked to imitate Pope. When traveling companies of actors appeared in any frontier zone, they usually included Shakespeare in their repertory, and when amateurs wanted to give something more substantial than the farces popular in church and school repertories, they, too, usually picked something from Shakespeare, preferably *The Merchant of Venice*.[9]

Elsewhere we have already observed the enduring popularity in the West of English and Scottish writers.

Sir Walter Scott and Robert Burns enjoyed a great vogue in the Middle West and later in the Far West. Byron was also tremendously popular, though some readers professed to be put off by his "wickedness." A few years ago, the lady dean of a Pacific Coast college made a fuss when an instructor commended *Don Juan* to the co-eds. Nevertheless, the smell of brimstone which clung to Byron only served to increase his fascination for Western readers. Paradoxically it was the good morality of Robert Southey and the virtuous sentimentality of Mrs. Felicia Hemans which made them favorites. Generations of Americans received their notions of the Plymouth settlers from reading Mrs. Hemans' "The Landing of the Pilgrim Fathers," which they later confirmed in Longfellow's "The Courtship of Miles Standish."

For a time Fenimore Cooper was acclaimed in the West as a rival of Scott and he did influence Western fiction to some degree, but he never achieved Scott's prestige. Cooper like many other American writers complained that the lack of an international copyright law repressed American literature.[10] When publishers could reprint any British writer without paying a cent for the privilege, they were not enthusiastic about native authors who demanded royalties. Though English writers might be flattered by the evidence of popularity in America, they were bitter when they calculated the loss to their pocketbooks. One reason for Charles Dickens' sour commentary in *The American Notes* was his realization of the financial loss from the piracy of his works. Not until 1891 was this condition improved. Whatever may have been the ethical considerations, the freedom to reprint British authors stimulated the circulation of British books in this country and helps to account for the long domination of English literature.

The impact of English literature was felt in some degree by thousands of Americans who never once in their lives owned or read a complete book by any writer, English or American. The influence came through schoolbooks, especially the readers which printed selections from poets, novelists, essayists, dramatists, and orators. Teachers believed in the efficacy of committing poetry to memory, and many a man and woman carried through life stanzas of poetry which they had memorized from the school readers. In many frontier schools, Friday afternoon was dedicated to oratory, with declamations by pupils of all ages. Most of the speeches were recitations taken from the reading books.

The concern of pressure groups, special interests, and patriots over the message which textbooks may carry to the young is well founded, for the propaganda value of schoolbooks is enormous. Whoever controls the material which goes into textbooks has a means of shaping the minds of the users of those books. During the whole of the period of settlement in this country, the textbooks used in the schools were permeated with piety and lessons of thrift, diligence, and sobriety, the characteristics of the seventeenth-century English middle class which found such fertile soil in the New World.

The early textbooks did not attempt to disguise their propaganda. For example, one book used in England and imported into the colonies made its purpose explicit in the title: *The Protestant Tutor, instructing Youth and Others, in the compleat method of Spelling, Reading, and Writing True English: Also discovering to them the Notorious Errors, Damnable Doctrines, and cruel Massacres of the bloody Papists, which England may expect from a Popish Successor* (*ca.* 1715).[11] Most schoolbooks did not emphasize religious bigotry so obviously, but the books having the widest circulation carried propaganda for Protestant piety. The most popular spelling book and elementary reader during the eighteenth century was compiled about 1740 by an Englishman, Thomas Dilworth, and bore the title *A New Guide to the English Tongue.* Dilworth also compiled an arithmetic called the *Schoolmaster's Assistant,* and other textbooks. So popular were these books that they were literally worn to pieces. The earliest Dilworth speller recorded in the Library of Congress is the twentieth edition of 1758. Part IV of the book was "An useful collection of sentences in prose and verse, divine, moral, and historical" and Part V consisted of "Forms of prayers for children on several occasions." [12] As children learned to spell and read they were supposed to imbibe lessons in good morality. Dilworth, like later textbook compilers, spelled out the "morals" of each selection in a sentence called "The Interpretation." This became standard technique in elementary reading books. Colonial Americans were brought up on Dilworth, and his textbooks, altered and adapted to suit changed conditions, continued in use until long after the Revolution.

Among the Puritans the elementary textbook which had the longest popularity was the famous *New England Primer*, probably first published in Boston about 1690.[13] For a century this book continued to be printed, sometimes under different titles and frequently with the material altered to suit the most recent compiler's fancy. Substantially it remained grimly Puritan in its moralizations and themes. The rhymes for each letter by which the alphabet was learned were frequently changed, but one remained constant because it carried the germ of Calvinistic theology: "In Adam's Fall, We sinned all." The poetic quality of the primer may be indicated by another rhyme for the letter "O": "Young Obadias, David, Josias, All were pious." The reading selections of the *New England Primer* included the Westminster Assembly's Shorter Catechism, described by Cotton Mather as "a little watering pot to shed good lessons." [14] During the eighteenth and early nineteenth centuries, it is estimated that at least three million copies of the primer were sold, and imitations of it appeared from time to time during the early years of the nineteenth century. In all of these books, the child's mind was bombarded with texts which stressed the imminence of death, the terrors of hell, and the necessity of piety as a means of escaping eternal punishment.

After the Revolution patriots began to worry about the Royalistic propaganda and the English slant of

Dilworth's *New Guide to the English Tongue* and other traditional English textbooks. Several highly conservative New England teachers and preachers saw their duty and hastened to supply the American market with suitable schoolbooks which would be at once conservatively Federalistic, patriotic, and soundly orthodox in religion. The first of these compilers was Noah Webster, a Yale graduate turned schoolmaster, who compiled a speller, grammar, and reader which he wanted to call "The American Instructor" but allowed President Ezra Stiles of Yale to christen with the more high-sounding title of *A Grammatical Institute of the English Language*, perhaps, it has been suggested, by analogy with Calvin's *Institutes*. The spelling book was the first to appear, in 1783, in an edition of 5,000 copies. For more than a half-century thereafter this book, commonly called the "blue-back speller," gave American boys and girls instruction in pronunciation and spelling. Webster sought to eliminate British forms of spelling and to substitute what he considered the best of his native dialect as the standard pronunciation of the United States. His grammar and reader were equally patriotic in their points of view and in the selection of material to glorify the Federalist position in politics.

A rival of Webster was Caleb Bingham, a Dartmouth graduate and later a Boston schoolmaster, who was as conservative in politics as in religion. A strict Congregationalist, he found the growing Unitarianism of Boston highly alarming, and he looked upon Jeffersonian republicanism as a wickedness imported from revolutionary and depraved France. His first textbook was a grammar and reader for girls but "proper for either sex" entitled *The Young Lady's Accidence* (1785). This was followed by *The American Preceptor* (1794) and *The Columbian Orator* (1797). All of these were characterized by their patriotic conservatism and their religious emphasis.

Webster and Bingham's books did not please all Americans, many of whom found it hard to accept the New England point of view. For example, they did not universally approve of what they described as the New England nasal twang which Webster sought to introduce as the standard of pronunciation for this country. For that reason they preferred a book by an Englishman, John Walker, who published in 1791 *A Critical Pronouncing Dictionary and Expositor of the English Language*. For the next two generations, Walker's work, and adaptations of it, competed with Webster and Bingham. Virginians preferred Walker because he was more elegant than Webster and gave them authority for such pronunciations as "gyarden" for "garden."

The post-Revolutionary reform of textbooks included geographies and histories which had to be revised to present a new orientation toward the United States. Jedidiah Morse, a Congregational preacher from Yale, wrote the most popular geographies. His first successful text was *Geography Made Easy* (1784), followed by *The American Geography* (1789) and various other works, including *A Compendious History of New England designed for schools and private families* (1804). Morse displayed an uncanny ability to teach geography with a Calvinistic slant and a New England orientation. His *Geography Made Easy* showed a concentration on the eastern United States which was natural enough for the times but it confirmed provincial notions which Westerners claim still dominate Eastern folklore. For example, Morse declared that "North America has no remarkably high mountains. The most considerable are those known under the general name of the Allegany Mountains." [15] I once heard a Californian standing in the shadow of Mt. Whitney remark that the average New Yorker had never heard of the Sierra Nevada and thought Bear Mountain the tallest peak in the land.

As the West developed a regional self-consciousness, it reacted against the New England school of textbook writers and demanded something more suitable for its own needs. William Holmes McGuffey was the answer to the West's prayer for fresher and more appropriate textbooks. McGuffey was a Presbyterian preacher of Scottish descent who had been born and brought up on the Ohio frontier. He attended Washington College in Western Pennsylvania and later taught school, preached, and lectured in Kentucky and Ohio. In 1826 he accepted an invitation from President Robert H. Bishop to become professor of languages at Miami University in Oxford, Ohio. Subsequently he was president of Cincinnati College and Ohio University at

Athens. In 1845 he left the Middle West and went to the University of Virginia as professor of moral philosophy, and there he remained for the rest of his active life.

While he was at Miami University, the Cincinnati publishing house of Truman and Smith persuaded him to prepare a series of reading books. The publishers wanted something more up-to-date and more in contact with the modern world than the school readers then available. Westerners on the whole were too optimistic to be content with tne doom-and-death motives which had frightened generations of children using the *New England Primer*. Even the Webster and Bingham readers were too provincial—and perhaps too Federalistic —for Western tastes.

McGuffey set to work and compiled a series of readers which swept the whole Western country and remained in vogue for the rest of the nineteenth century. Even yet elderly men and women remember McGuffey's *Eclectic Readers* with nostalgia, and think that America would be a better place if we could go back to the simple virtues commended in his books. On July 28, 1952, *Time Magazine* reported a meeting during the previous week of 300 members of the McGuffey Society to dedicate a McGuffey Museum at Miami University. "Before they finally faded from U. S. schools in the early 1900's," *Time* asserted, "the six *Eclectic Readers* and the *Eclectic Spelling Book* (edited by Brother Alexander McGuffey) sold some 130 million copies, probably had more influence on U. S. literary

tastes and moral standards than any other book except
the Bible."

McGuffey's *First* and *Second Reader* appeared in
1836, the *Third* and *Fourth Reader* in 1837, the *Fifth
Reader* in 1844, the *Eclectic Spelling Book* in 1846, and
the *Sixth Reader* in 1857. The various books went
through innumerable editions. The Miami University
Museum possesses nearly 400 separate editions including translations, one into Japanese. The McGuffey
Readers appealed to the nineteenth century because
they shrewdly combined good morality, patriotism, and
faith in material progress. They brought into modern
focus the middle-class ideas and aspirations which had
been gathering strength since the seventeenth century.
Benjamin Franklin in the wisdom of Poor Richard published in his successive almanacs had done the same
thing in the eighteenth century and Franklin has had
more influence than any other American philosopher.
With many of the same ideas McGuffey successfully
adapted his textbooks to the time-spirit of his own
age.

McGuffey succeeded in making his books interesting and gave them a universal appeal. In contrast with
the grim lessons of hell-fire and damnation in the *New
England Primer* and other Puritan texts, McGuffey
taught a humane morality; compassion and a forgiving
spirit were held up as virtues. The *First* and *Second
Reader* were full of moralized anecdotes and tales, but
they dealt with everyday children in situations com-

prehensible to a child. The *Second Reader,* for example, retold Parson Weems' story of George Washington and the cherry tree, and fixed that tale firmly in American folklore. The *Third Reader* had selections from the Bible, incidents from the life of Napoleon, a homely little explanation of "How a Fly Walks on the Ceiling," and other selections designed to interest and instruct the pupil. Its poetical selections included "The Old Oaken Bucket." The *Fourth, Fifth* and *Sixth Reader* were heavily laden with excerpts from the best English authors, but selections designed to teach sound moral attitudes, thrift, diligence, sobriety, and patriotism.

McGuffey gave his *Fifth Reader* the additional title of *Rhetorical Guide . . . Containing Elegant Extracts in Prose and Poetry: With Copious Rules and Rhetorical Exercises.* It was plainly designed to supply material for recitations and it was filled with "elegant" pieces which remained continuously popular for generations. Shakespeare supplied more passages than any other single author, and, lest the reader miss the proper meaning, the headings were explicit. For instance, a dialogue between Cassio and Iago from *Othello* was entitled "Folly of Intoxication." After Shakespeare came Scott, Byron, Thomas Gray, Mrs. Hemans, Southey, Burke, Lord Chatham, Goldsmith, Dr. Johnson, Macaulay, and a host of others including anonymous excerpts from the *Edinburgh Review.* American authors included Patrick Henry, Daniel Webster, Longfellow, Bryant, Irving, Edward Everett, and other orators and poets. From this book children learned Mark Antony's oration over dead Caesar, Hamlet's soliloquy, Gray's "Elegy," Scott's "Lochinvar," Mrs. Hemans' "Landing of the Pilgrim Fathers," or some other piece which took their fancy, and they declaimed their speeches before admiring friends and neighbors. Such selections became a part of the literary inheritance of the West and many schoolchildren got a taste for reading which led them to seek a further acquaintance with the writings of worth-while authors.

McGuffey never let his pupils overlook the social significance of literature. He was careful to include in the *Fifth Reader* a selection from Blackstone's *Commentaries* on the "Origin of Property," and the last prose extract in the volume is an essay entitled "God Blesses the Industrious." The final item is Psalm 37 which promises God's favor to the righteous and is full of apt lessons such as "The wicked borroweth and payeth not again; But the righteous showeth mercy and giveth." Often quoted was the verse which many a child probably memorized from McGuffey instead of the Book of Psalms:

> I have been young, and now am old,
> Yet have I not seen the righteous forsaken,
> Nor his seed begging bread.
> He is ever merciful and lendeth,
> And his seed is blessed.

This was a cheerful note to close upon, quite at variance with the morbid preoccupation with death and damnation in older texts and much more in keeping with the optimistic and hopeful West. McGuffey also displayed a new spirit of toleration. In his *Fifth Reader* he included a moving passage from Henry Grattan's "Speech on the Catholic Question" in which Grattan defended the rights of Irish Catholics.

The political philosophy taught in McGuffey was conservative but it had an orientation entirely different from the conservatism of the older Federalist textbooks. McGuffey's books were nationalistic in tone with a strong emphasis on the Great West as a land of opportunity where hard work and virtuous behavior would have their material rewards. "The conception of the West one gets from the early lessons of the McGuffey readers, then," one commentator observes, "is that of a vast world set apart by nature for the prosperity and culture of the citizens who dared venture into her vast lands." [16] The books stressed patriotism and included ample passages on popular heroes, Washington in particular. The implication of many of the passages is that American heroes have inherited the virtues of the past, from ancient Greece to modern England, and that Americans in time will surpass all other peoples in merit. Such doctrines were congenial to an ambitious frontier society pushing forward to claim an inland empire. That these teachings have left a heritage of nationalistic isolationism in the Middle West is obvious.

McGuffey has been accused of neglecting esthetic considerations in his textbooks. "Emphatic in the glorification of moral, religious, and purely practical concerns, and aiding thus on one side of cultural growth," one critic comments, "they failed almost completely to stir the imagination, and they scarcely suggested the possibility of enjoyment in music and the fine arts or in literature freed of too immediate didactic purpose." [17] No self-conscious estheticism is evident in the *Readers,* it is true, but esthetic interest was implicit in the quality of numerous selections from the best authors. There is ample testimony too that they stirred the imagination of boys and girls in the West. Hamlin Garland, for example, in *A Son of the Middle Border* pays this tribute to the civilizing quality of McGuffey's *Readers:* "Our readers were almost the only counterchecks to the current of vulgarity and baseness which ran through the talk of the older boys, and I wish to acknowledge my deep obligation to Professor McGuffey, whoever he may have been, for the dignity and literary grace of his selections. From the pages of his readers I learned to know and love the poems of Scott, Byron, Southey, Wordsworth, and a long line of English masters. I got my first taste of Shakespeare from the selected scenes which I read in these books." [18] Garland's experience in the frontier zone of the West was that of thousands of youngsters who did not find that McGuffey's didacticism destroyed the beauty of the literary passages which he made available to them.

The influence of McGuffey's *Readers* on the civilization of the West—and upon other parts of the country, for that matter—cannot be calculated, but certainly few other textbooks had such a continuous impact upon the minds of Americans. During the first year of publication in 1836 Truman and Smith sold more than 20,000 copies of the *First Reader*. Within six years, the sales of the books had reached 700,000 copies, and before the end of the century, at least 122,000,000 had been sold. Most of these *Readers* were used over and over until they were worn to shreds. Today early issues are scarce and hard to come by. How many millions of Americans received their fundamental education out of these books, no man can say. But most of the West used these *Readers*, which supplied solid meat and substance for their minds. Whether one accepts today the social philosophy implicit in McGuffey, it would be hard to deny the integrity and high literary quality of most of the selections. By comparison much of the material found in analogous school texts today is sentimental and ill-written rubbish.

The nationalistic "Americanism" implicit in McGuffey's *Readers* is now acclaimed by certain super-patriots as a gospel of primitive virtue to which we ought to return. Some of our isolationists who hold with these views are perhaps unaware that McGuffey, for all of his nationalistic fervor, represents an almost pure strain of British culture modified only by transplantation to the New World. Even the selections from American writers included in his texts are mostly from authors who wrote in imitation of British models. The "old Americanism" of McGuffey taught in countless schools of the West attempted to remodel the sons and daughters of immigrants from foreign lands into our inherited Anglo-Saxon pattern. The success of the schools was phenomenal. The second generation from Scandinavia, Germany, Poland, Russia, Italy, Yugoslavia, or even Japan and China accepted the English language as their own, and began to look upon traditional English literature as their cultural inheritance. Polish schoolboys declaimed Mark Antony's oration over Caesar, Italian schoolgirls recited Portia's speech on mercy, and all read Scott's *Ivanhoe*, Burke's *Speech on the Conciliation of the Colonies*, and innumerable other British classics. The "Americanization" of nineteenth-century immigrants on the frontier largely consisted in giving them a common school education in the backgrounds of English literature.

As we have already observed, the leaders of the westward movement were convinced of the value of education and lost no time in establishing schools and colleges on the successive frontiers. In the nineteenth century, many Americans were beginning to substitute a faith in popular education for their former preoccupation with revealed religion. Public education, indeed, became a religion, and Americans looked to it as the way to social salvation. The most intense periods of westward expansion coincided with the growth of faith in education, a fact which helps to explain the multiplication of schools and colleges in the West. These institutions were potent instruments in transmitting to the frontier the older cultural traditions of the Anglo-Saxon Eastern seaboard.

In addition to the normal activities of the schools, they provided a cultural center for their communities.

The present-day city-dweller has no conception of the place the school occupied in the social life of the rural districts. There literary societies met; there the first rudimentary public library was housed; there the people met for discussion and debate; there came the spellbinding lecturer or the itinerant "professor" with his electrical machine and demonstration of scientific wonders. When a raw Western town could boast a college, the populace of the surrounding country flocked to its "attractions." Lyceum programs were part of the college's contribution to general education. Oratorical contests among the students drew crowds as athletic events do now. Concerts by glee clubs, college choirs, and orchestras were usually the only serious music available outside of the church. Local historical and scientific societies might find inspiration in the college faculty and a place to meet in the college halls. The schoolhouse and the college provided a stage for amateur theatricals or for the traveling company which occasionally brought drama to Western communities.

In one noteworthy respect, the academies and colleges which flourished in the West were more advanced than their Eastern counterparts. They quickly realized that women had an equal right to the same kind of education available to men and they threw their doors open to women. Oberlin, Antioch, the University of Michigan, the University of Wisconsin, and numerous other institutions in the West allowed women the same educational privileges as men. Coeducation was accepted as a sensible, an economical, and a just system.

It was hard to explain to a pioneer woman who could endure the toil and hardships of trail or field that she was physically incapable of enduring the strain of a masculine education. Since women necessarily bore a heavy burden of responsibility in civilizing the West, this enlightened attitude toward her education was important.

The difference of attitude in the East toward the education of women is revealing. Long after women in the West were happily pursuing standard liberal arts and professional courses on a full equality with men, Eastern pedagogues were learnedly asserting that females were unfit for the rigors of severe mental discipline. Some of the opponents of higher education for women claimed to be inspired by a chivalrous desire to protect the weaker sex from the corrosive and destructive effects of learning. In 1874 Dr. Edward H. Clarke, professor at Harvard, distilled the essence of his wisdom into a book which he called *Sex in Education, or a Fair Chance for Girls*. Dr. Clarke had surveyed the prospect of girls competing with men in colleges and was against it. It would not be fair to the girls. The struggle would be too severe for their slender abilities and they would fall victims of consumption, or worse, of mental disorders. Furthermore, abstract learning would unfit them for their essential duties as wives and mothers. When medical men pointed out that their experience did not bear out Dr. Clarke's contentions, the professor answered with a second volume in 1880 entitled *Building a Brain*. He clearly demonstrated the folly of trying to nourish a woman's mind on the arts and sciences hitherto reserved to men. Persistence in this endeavor would lead to certain disaster, he insisted. Men would not want to marry pallid she-scholars, for even if women survived four years of college, they would be exhausted and unfit for homemaking. Fifty years of higher education for women, Dr. Clarke warned, would ruin the nation, and American men would have to send across the Atlantic for fit wives.

Meanwhile the West was busily educating its women and observing no dangerous effects. Marriages appeared to be just as successful as elsewhere, and if anything, women were happier and more active in good works. They taught schools, organized literary clubs, created lending libraries, sponsored lyceum courses, and took an active and intelligent part in every movement for cultural uplift. So convinced was the West in woman's fitness to have an equal responsibility in society that Wyoming in 1869 and Utah in 1870 set an example to the rest of the country by permitting women to vote.

The reform movements of the early nineteenth century first taught American women to realize their power through organization, but even before this, women had joined together in charitable enterprises, missionary societies, and mutual improvement groups. The temperance and anti-slavery agitations enlisted women in the cause, and before the middle of the century women were beginning to form clubs to foster a variety of activities. By the middle of the century, cultural improvement was already a prime objective, and from that time onward, the most progressive Western towns were boasting of their ladies' literary societies. The men sometimes poked fun at the highfalutin' pretensions of their wives, but the women went ahead with their papers on Shakespeare, Sir Walter Scott, or some other theme deemed sufficiently improving.

Masculine clubs, it is true, had existed since colonial days, and some were devoted to intellectual concerns. Several Western towns, for example, had historical or scientific societies. But literary culture with a capital C became the main preoccupation of the Western women's clubs. The sophisticated today may laugh at their aspirations and their superficiality, but these organized women's groups undoubtedly performed an important service in stimulating the study of both history and literature. Perhaps the earliest of the Western women's clubs was one reported in Robert Owen's socialist colony at New Harmony, Indiana, in 1825 as the Female Social Society. Only a few scanty records tell of its purposes. More interesting was a ladies' literary society organized at Bloomington in 1841. It bore the name of Edgeworthalian, after Maria Edgeworth, English author of moral tales, and Thalia, the muse of pastoral poetry, surely a significant name for a self-improvement society in a country town. An applicant for membership was required to sign a formal statement beginning: "The undersigned, feeling the need of something to stimulate her mental and moral culture, and believing the means may be the concentration in a literary society or body associated expressly to impart and receive instruction, hereby offers herself a candidate for the honor of membership in the Edgeworthalian Society." [19] The club proposed to collect "a library of select books" and in addition to literary discussions, debated such questions as: "Which was the most blameworthy in the original transgression, Adam or Eve?"

Innumerable women's clubs busily set to work to civilize the West. One of the earliest was the Ladies' Educational Association of Jacksonville, Illinois, established in 1833. The wives of the pioneer missionaries to Oregon in 1838 organized the Maternal Association under the leadership of Mrs. Marcus Whitman. The club came to an end with the Whitman massacre in 1847. Prototype of the modern federated woman's club was the Minerva Club organized at New Harmony, Indiana, in 1857 by a granddaughter of Robert Owen who wanted to bring European culture to the Middle West. Other clubs were less ambitious but more practical. In 1852 the few women in the raw town of Kalamazoo, Michigan, formed the Ladies' Library Association. They not only established a public library—"as a means of educating the people and forming a taste for reading" [20]—but they met as a club to analyze and discuss the books. In scores of communities women's clubs devoted their efforts to the study of English history and English literature. The Ladies' History Club of Sioux Falls, South Dakota, organized in 1879 for the purpose of studying English history.[21] Ten years later, the Woman's Club of Watertown, South Dakota, took as its first task a study of English history and followed this with a course of reading in American history. The Zetetic Club of Weeping Water, Nebraska, founded in 1884, devoted itself to the history of the Reformation, Elizabethan England, and finally graduated into the French Revolution. After that it devoted two years to reading Shakespeare. Indeed, Shakespeare was the most popular single author with the frontier clubs. The Woman's Club of Sleepy Eye, Minnesota, chose Shakespeare as its main theme but followed with history. The women of Idaho Springs, Idaho, formed a Shakespeare Club as early as 1888. Moscow, Idaho, soon had a Ladies' Historical Society and other Idaho towns were busy studying history, Shakespeare, and other cultural subjects. Butte, Montana, had a Homer Club which read Greek history and translations of the *Iliad* and the *Odyssey* before turning to early American history.

In the Iowa prairie communities in the 1850's women organized reading circles in their homes and these groups proved so successful that men were occasionally admitted. In 1856 Edward Everett delivered a lecture in Dubuque which moved the community to found a library, organize a lecture program, and continue to read. A chronicler of the Conversational Club of Dubuque explains the working of this ferment: "There had been from 1857, the year of the financial depression, a growing desire among women to read. The lurid political horizon portended storms; women felt the need of council [sic] in their study, to confer together on literary, religious, historical, and social topics." [22] About the same time women's clubs in Kansas were also studying literature and history and trying to improve themselves in similar fashion. Some of them appear to have gone somewhat farther afield than their sisters in Iowa, for listed in topics of papers are such themes as "A Higher Life for Hindu Women," and "Ten Minutes with the Russians." [23]

The zeal for self-improvement which ran through Americans like a virus in the nineteenth century manifested itself in an exaggerated devotion to the lecture platform as an agency of intellectual and spiritual uplift. The West especially took itinerant lecturers to its bosom and even yet displays an insatiable appetite for the spoken word. California is still a paradise for public speakers on every conceivable subject. Glib speakers accumulate fortunes reviewing books for women's clubs, and I knew one woman who had a well-paying circuit in Southern California where she reviewed the current magazine digests, thus saving Californians much mental exertion. Faith in the lecture platform took hold in the 1830's as a sequel to the success of the lyceum movement begun in Connecticut in 1836 by Josiah Holbrook, who thought he could educate the vast uninstructed public with courses of lectures. He announced his own readiness to speak on "history, art, science, and public questions" and presently organized the National American Lyceum designed to carry cultural salvation to the country. By 1830 lyceum courses were being offered in Cincinnati, and within a few years the plan had spread throughout the West. Before the Civil War hundreds of lyceum courses were taking lecturers to the most distant frontier outposts. The public turned out in droves. In the days before the motion picture, radio, and television, the itinerant lecturer furnished both edification and entertainment.

Upon Cincinnati, an important cultural center of the growing West, lecturers early began to converge. Literature, history, and science were the subjects most popular. At its Western Museum, the public might hear discourses on birds, minerals, astronomy, physiology, or phrenology. In 1828 Dr. John Locke gave a series of talks on natural philosophy designed to appeal to the common understanding. In 1833, Calvin E. Stowe lectured on the "History of Letters" and James Hall spoke on the "Importance of Forming a First Class Library in Cincinnati." His words were so effective that two years later Cincinnati organized the Young Men's Mercantile Library Association which sponsored lectures as a means of instructing the general public. The Library Association's taste was catholic, for in the next few years it brought to Cincinnati such diverse personalities as Robert Dale Owen, Horace Greeley, Alexander Campbell, Cassius M. Clay, George W. Curtis, Bayard Taylor, Oliver Wendell Holmes, Wendell Phillips, and Edward Everett. Everett was one of the most notable spellbinders of the day and was enormously popular.

His patriotism apparently ran away with his normal prudence in 1857 when he gave his famous lecture on George Washington in Cincinnati "free of charge." [24] Everett could afford one free lecture, for he had been saving the soul of the West by his eloquence for nearly thirty years—usually at a substantial fee.

An editorial in *The Herald of Truth* for February 1848 commending uplifting speakers in Cincinnati, may be taken as a measure of the West's general attitude toward the lecture platform: "There is at this time an unusual degree of intellectual activity in Cincinnati," the *Herald* points out. "The Young Men's Mercantile Library Association have a course of very able lectures in progress which are attended by a large portion of the first minds in the city. Then there is a course of lectures on early American eloquence by Rev. E. L. Magoon; on constitutional history by William Green, Esq.; and on the duties and responsibilities of the American citizen by Rev. C. B. Boynton; which afford a rich treat to the intellectual and moral man. Then we have a debate on phrenology and philosophy by and between Dr. N. L. Rice and Prof. J. R. Buchanan, which call out large crowds to hear great principles discussed, such as whether phrenology teaches a system of fatalism, and whether philosophy and Christianity are consistent with each other. Then we have recently had a course of lectures by F. W. Thomas, author of the popular novel *Clinton Bradshaw*, on those illuminated Methodist seers, Wesley, Whitfield, and Somerfield, which attracted so much attention as to induce a request for

their repetition. These are only some of the most prominent of the substantial mental doings of the city at
present. There is nothing so important as keeping up a
high mental activity so that the great cause of truth
may be advanced, goodness increased, and happiness
promoted." [25]

If formal lectures could promote happiness, the West
was determined to be a paradise. In the fall of 1854
the periodical, *The Genius of the West,* announced
with pride that "we are informed that nearly every
town in the West will this winter have one or more
courses of lectures." And the journal printed two lists,
one of Eastern lecturers and another of native Westerners. The Eastern list included Emerson, Thoreau,
Wendell Phillips, and Henry Ward Beecher. Their
prices ranged from $40 to $75 per lecture. The Western
list included local professors, preachers, lawyers, and
one librarian, the state librarian of Ohio. They came
cheap and would talk for as little as $15 to $25.[26]

So taken were certain Ohio citizens with the promise
of the lyceum that in 1837 they established a lyceum
seminary at Berea, Ohio, which was designed to combine manual labor and inspirational talk in the right
proportions to be both financially profitable and intel-
lectually beneficial. Josiah Holbrook, father of the lyceum movement, announced the lofty aims of lyceum-
promoted seminaries of the Berea type: "The general
plan of lyceums has ever contemplated within every
county or other moderate district a manual labor and
self-supporting school which should furnish to its pupils

advantages equal to those in our colleges for general literature and science, and much superior for practical business education to those of any institution in our country." [27] In their enthusiasm for lyceum lecture courses, some Westerners thought they might supply instruction to areas which could not be reached by schools. On the Illinois frontier in the 1830's it was believed that itinerant lecturers might furnish weekly instruction to children as well as adults and thus cover a wide circuit. In 1852 the Governor of Ohio requested the legislature to appropriate funds to support lyceums and literary associations "to prevent dissipation by the desertion of places tending to immoralities and cause young men to store their minds with useful knowledge and elevate themselves in their own self-dignity and self-respect." [28] The lyceums frequently resulted in the formation of reading clubs and the establishment of community libraries.

The lecturers who flocked to the West brought messages of infinite variety. Emerson, for example, talked on "Natural Aristocracy," "Eloquence," "England," "Books," "The Spirit of the Times," and many other themes. Though he had a loyal following, he was not completely successful because he provided more inspiration than information, and the practical West wanted facts, and preferably facts mixed with entertainment. "The persistent criticism of Emerson was that he left his audience with only a meager fund of immediately useful knowledge," one historian comments. [29] Henry Giles, a Unitarian preacher without a pulpit, gained favor with a series of lectures on "The Comic Powers of Shakespeare," and on *Don Quixote*. Edward P. Whipple lectured alternately on "The American Mind" and "The English Mind." Bronson Alcott conceived the notion of stimulating Socratic conversations between the lecturer and the public, but Western audiences were lukewarm to the idea and showed no enthusiasm for Alcott's own "Orphic Sayings." Nevertheless, after a discussion of Hegel in St. Louis, Alcott himself was moved to remark that "Western minds and audiences were in many respects superior to those of New England." [30] Lectures on history, literature, science, or behavior if eloquently presented or interspersed with entertaining anecdotes usually attracted crowds. "The business of lecturing," Theodore Parker observed, "is an original American contrivance for educating the people. The world has nothing like it. In it are combined the best things of the church and of the college, with some of the fun of the theatre." [31]

American contrivance though the lecture platform might be, Englishmen soon heard that it was a profitable business, and for a century the English lecturer was a common if not always a successful evangel of culture in the West. The Englishman's condescension toward American "colonials"—as he often made them appear—was a constant source of irritation and did much to unsweeten Anglo-American relations, though Americans continued to pay fees to hear Englishmen describe Yankee cultural shortcomings. The persistence of the English lecturer in the West is one of the curious phenomena of the nineteenth and early twentieth centuries. Perhaps the English lecturer's hold on the public lay in the subconscious feeling on the part of Americans that the Englishman had something to impart which was culturally uplifting, however unpalatable it might be to take.

Among the many agencies which helped to civilize the moving frontier, the country newspaper occupied an important place. The editor might be a local lawyer, teacher, preacher, or self-educated printer. In any case, the paper he published reflected his personality and views in a way unknown today when we depend upon huge, impersonal, metropolitan papers. The editor was close to the people; he knew most of them with some degree of intimacy; he had a stake in the community; and he usually was the leader of progressive enterprises to improve his town and county. He had to be a man of tenacity and courage. If he did not speak his mind, his clientele lost respect for him; if he was too outspoken, he might find himself in danger of life and limb. Legend attributes to the necessity of making a hurried exit the newspaperman's habit of wearing his hat at his desk. The country editor might not have a polished education himself but he was usually the advocate of schools, libraries, lecture programs, and other means of bringing literacy and enlightenment to the people. He might print excerpts from books and magazines, and his paper was sometimes the only reading matter available in backwoods areas. The country newspaper shaped opinion and provided material to feed minds which might otherwise have starved for want of literate material.

The newspaper also made many indirect contributions to the stimulation of intellectual activity. For example, local antiquarians used the columns of the country papers to report the history of their localities, and the activities of one or two amateur historians and self-made anthropologists sometimes resulted in the organization of historical and scientific societies. The papers were, of course, open to contributors who felt the creative urge, for the editor was frequently not the only author in the community. An appalling number of people are inspired to write verse when under the influence of a great emotion, and the country papers published more than enough of the poetic efforts of their patrons. Some was lachrymose; some was satirical or sentimental; and most was very bad. But the paper was the instrumentality of a beneficial literary catharsis.

From a purely utilitarian point of view the country papers served to bring order into chaotic communities in the early stages of frontier development. For example, they were the one practical means of disseminating government notices and legal information. Indeed, printing legal notices for the county government provided a subsidy which kept many papers going. Without the newspapers, the procedure of civilizing the frontier would have been slower and harder.

The maintenance of contact with the world which the Western pioneers had left behind them was one of the most important functions of country newspapers.

The material which they printed might not be profound or highly important either for its literary or news value, but it was a link with a larger literate world. The humble country newspaper was both a transmitter of information and a conservator of traditional culture.

An infinite variety of agencies, from parsons in their pulpits to shirt-sleeved editors of ragged little weekly papers, labored to bring law and order, decency, learning, and cultivation to a succession of frontier regions beginning with the Atlantic littoral in the seventeenth century and ending with the Pacific Coast and the interior Great Basin in the nineteenth. The task of molding an inchoate mass of people from many nations and races into something approaching a homogeneous society was not easy, but miraculously it succeeded.

We used to be fond of talking about the melting pot of America. But what did the component elements melt into? Into something called an American, and that American had a prototype across the seas who was responsible for the American's language, his basic laws, his fundamental liberties, and much of his manners, customs, and social attitudes. That prototype was British, and primarily English. The English tradition was the strongest element of civilization on the successive frontiers. It had an incredible power of assimilation and transmutation. At the end of the eighteenth century a Frenchman naturalized in New York, Hector St. John De Crèvecoeur, wrote a famous essay asking the question, "What Is an American?" And he answered by declaring that "the American is a new man" assimilated from a "mixture of English, Scotch, Irish, French, Dutch, German, and Swedes. From this promiscuous breed that race now called Americans have arisen." [32] Two significant factors were responsible for the assimilation of these people into the new American: the economic opportunities of the young country and the cultural traditions of the predominant English. Whatever the national and racial origins of American immigrants might be, within two generations, most Americans so reflected English ideas and attitudes that many of them might have passed for Englishmen.

In a book full of salty wisdom entitled *Our English Heritage,* Gerald W. Johnson recognized the assimilative quality of the English tradition and pointed out the nature of our inheritance. "The England that still holds a powerful grip upon the thoughts and acts of the American people, including those of non-English origin," writes Mr. Johnson, "is not the realm of the English king, nor the institutions created by the English people. It is nothing so tangible, nothing definable in materialistic terms. It is a story, partly history, partly legend, largely poetry and drama." [33] It is the story of the plain man's struggle and rise from serfdom to the greatest liberty under law that any man has ever known. It is also an inheritance of practicality from a nation of shop-keepers who taught us that commerce is honorable and that fair play in business is part of the code of decent men. Locke, Hobbes, and Herbert Spencer all contributed their theories to English philosophy which has influenced us, but Mr. Johnson observes quite correctly that most of us know nothing of them directly. "The English philosophy that still sways the thoughts and acts of millions [of Americans] who never saw inside of a college is none of these," Mr. Johnson adds. "It is English faith in gradualism linked with compromise, English faith in ability as at least equal to heredity, and English faith in commerce as a better instrument of conquest than war." [34] The pragmatism which permeates American thought is essentially an inheritance from middle-class England.

A quality in us that our British brethren today find hard to bear is the conviction, with its corollaries, that we are God's chosen people. We are loud in the assertion that this is God's country; that our standard of living is the greatest blessing of mankind, and that universal bliss will come when the rest of the world has as many refrigerators, washing machines, and television sets as we possess; that the American constitution is the world's finest instrument of government; and that we are called upon to export our kind of civilization to all mankind. But this quality too is an inheritance from the British. Manifest Destiny was not an invention of President Polk and his generation or of any American, for that matter. Seventeenth-century English Puritans were convinced that they were God's saints destined to inherit this world and the next. Successive generations of the British were certain that God spoke English, and they heard a clear call to go out to the ends of the earth, to sell their goods, to bear the white man's burden, to rule the inefficient, and to spread their civilization. Americans expanding westward in the nineteenth century merely fell into a normal practice and devised a slogan to justify their actions.

For better or for worse, we have inherited the fundamental qualities in our culture from the British. For that reason we need to take a long perspective of our history, a perspective which views America from at least the period of the first Tudor monarchs and lets us see the gradual development of our common civilization, its transmission across the Atlantic, and its expansion and modification as it was adapted to conditions in the Western Hemisphere. We should not overlook other influences which have affected American life, influences from France, Holland, Spain, Germany, Scandinavia, and the rest of Europe, and also influences from Asia and Africa. But we must always remember that such was the vigor of British culture that it assimilated all others. That is not to say that we have been transmogrified into Englishmen, or that we are even Anglophile in sentiment. But we cannot escape an inheritance which has given us some of our sturdiest and most lasting qualities.

Notes

CHAPTER I

1. The realization that we are in danger of forgetting the tremendous force of the British tradition prompted Gerald W. Johnson to write *Our English Heritage* (Philadelphia, 1949). Pointing out the uncertain—or at least, non-English—background of the American people, Johnson remarks (pp. 230-231): "From this uncertainty has sprung in recent years a theory that since the country is no longer predominantly English, therefore it isn't English at all, or not to any important extent. It is a theory held tenaciously and hopefully by all who for highly emotional or severely rational reasons consider English influence derogatory to the country. Statistically and theoretically there is a good deal to support it. . . . But there is an imponderable factor that doesn't appear in statistical tables. It is the English power of transmutation, which is very considerable indeed, the indefinable process whereby a Swedish-French-Italian-Scottish-Flemish-Dutch combination touched by English influence may become so remarkably like an Englishman as to command the enthusiastic loyalty of the English." And Mr. Johnson adds: "It does not follow that when an American affected by this power of transmutation, takes on some English coloration he is necessarily improved. We assimilate their bad qualities as well as the better ones."

Our departures from the English norm are indicated or implied by Denis W. Brogan, *The American Character* (New York, 1944).

Dixon Ryan Fox's essay, "Civilization in Transit," in the volume *Ideas in Motion* (New York, 1935) is a useful introduction to the problem of the movement of cultural impulses across the continent.

2. Louis B. Wright, *The First Gentlemen of Virginia* (San Marino, Calif., 1936), p. 121.

3. *Ibid.*, p. 99.

4. Marcus W. Jernegan, *Laboring and Dependent Classes in Colonial America, 1607-1783* (Chicago, 1931), p. 49.

5. Wright, *First Gentlemen of Virginia*, p. 230.

6. *The Secret Diary of William Byrd of Westover, 1709-1712.* Ed. by Louis B. Wright and Marion Tinling (Richmond, Va., 1941), p. 361.

7. Quoted from *The First Gentlemen of Virginia*, p. 165.

8. *Ibid.*, p. 173.

9. William K. Boyd (ed.), *William Byrd's Histories of the Dividing Line Betwixt Virginia and North Carolina* (Raleigh, N. C., 1929), p. 92.

10. Arnold J. Toynbee, *A Study of History.* Abridgement of Volumes I-VI by D. C. Somervell (New York and London, 1947), pp. 149, 465.

11. Quoted from the text of *New Englands First Fruits* (1643), reprinted in Samuel E. Morison, *The Founding of Harvard College* (Cambridge, 1935), p. 432.

12. Henry F. Waters, "Instructions for Emigrants from Essex County, Mass., to South Carolina, 1697," *New England Historical and Genealogical Register*, XXX (1876), 64-67.

13. Cf. Louis B. Wright, "The Purposeful Reading of Our Colonial Ancestors," *E L H, A Journal of English Literary History*, IV (1937), 85-111.

14. *Diary of Cotton Mather, 1681-1708, Collections of the Massachusetts Historical Society*, 7th Ser., VII (1911), 65.

15. *Ibid.*, VIII (1912), 242. Entry for September 27, 1713.

16. *Collections of the Massachusetts Historical Society*, 5th Ser., I (1871), 259.

17. This theme is treated at greater length in Louis B. Wright, "The Westward Advance of the Atlantic Frontier," *The Huntington Library Quarterly*, XI (1948), 261-275.

18. Quoted by Wayland F. Dunaway, *The Scotch-Irish in Colonial Pennsylvania* (Chapel Hill, N. C., 1944), p. 220.

19. Thomas J. Wertenbaker, *Princeton, 1746-1896* (Princeton, N. J., 1946), p. 20.

20. Samuel E. Morison, *The Puritan Pronaos* (New York, 1936), p. 149.

21. Louis B. Wright, "Franklin's Legacy to the Gilded Age," *The Virginia Quarterly Review,* XX (1946), 268-279.

CHAPTER II

1. Daniel Drake, *Pioneer Life in Kentucky, 1785-1800.* Ed. by Emmet F. Horine (New York, 1948), p. 180.

2. *Ibid.,* pp. 189-190.

3. *Ibid.,* p. 193.

4. *Ibid.,* p. 194.

5. *Ibid.,* p. 8.

6. *Ibid.,* p. 161.

7. *Ibid.,* pp. 162-166.

8. *Ibid.,* p. 168.

9. Cf. James M. Miller, *The Genesis of Western Culture. The Upper Ohio Valley, 1800-1825. Ohio Historical Collections,* IX (Columbus, 1938), 38-40; Ralph Leslie Rusk, *The Literature of the Middle Western Frontier* (New York, 1926), I, 14-22.

10. Quoted by R. E. Banta, *The Ohio. Rivers of America Series* (New York, 1949), p. 409.

11. Thomas D. Clark, *A History of Kentucky* (New York, 1937), p. 303.

12. Quoted, *ibid.,* p. 305.

13. *Ibid.,* pp. 309-310.

14. Quoted by James H. Rodabaugh, *Robert Hamilton Bishop. Ohio Historical Collections,* IV (Columbus, 1935), 28.

15. *Ibid.,* p. 29.

16. Quoted, *ibid.,* p. 30.

17. Quoted by Charles R. Staples, *The History of Pioneer Lexington Ky. 1779-1806* (Lexington, 1939), pp. 245-246, from Thomas Ashe's *Travels in America in 1806.*

18. Clark, *History of Kentucky,* p. 314.

19. *Ibid.,* p. 339. See also Willard R. Jillson, *The Newspapers and Periodicals of Frankfort, Kentucky, 1795-1945* (Frankfort, 1945), pp. 4-5.

20. The amazing variety of publications printed in early

Kentucky may be seen in Douglas McMurtrie, *American Imprints Inventory, No. 5 Check List of Kentucky Imprints, 1787-1810* and *No. 6 Check List of Kentucky Imprints, 1811-1820* (Louisville, 1939).

21. Clark, *History of Kentucky*, p. 181.

22. Willard R. Jillson, *Early Kentucky Literature, 1750-1840* (Frankfort, 1932), pp. 41-47.

23. Quoted by John Wilson Townsend, *Kentucky in American Letters, 1784-1912* (Cedar Rapids, Iowa, 1913), pp. 22-23.

24. Clark, *History of I entucky*, p. 359.

25. Staples, *Pioneer Lexington*, p. 226.

26. Elizabeth Norton, "The Old Library of Transylvania College," *The History Quarterly Published Quarterly by the Filson Club and the University of Louisville*, I (1926-27), 122-133.

27. Staples, *Pioneer Lexington*, p. 146.

28. Ralph Leslie Rusk, *The Literature of the Middle Western Frontier* (New York, 1925), II, 4.

29. Robert G. Cleland, *This Reckless Breed of Men* (New York, 1950), p. 49.

30. Quoted by Staples, *Pioneer Lexington*, pp. 260-267.

31. Clark, *History of Kentucky*, p. 391.

32. *Ibid.*, p. 104.

33. Rusk, *Literature*, I, 354 ff.

34. *Ibid.*, I, 413-414.

35. Drake, *Pioneer Life*, p. 195.

CHAPTER III

1. Solon J. Buck and Elizabeth H. Buck, *The Planting of Civilization in Western Pennsylvania* (Pittsburgh, 1939), pp. 215-217.

2. Fortescue Cuming, *Sketches of a Tour to the Western Country* (Pittsburgh, 1810) in Reuben Thwaites (ed.), *Early Western Travels* (Cleveland, 1904), IV, 246.

3. Buck, *Planting of Civilization*, p. 385.

4. *Ibid.*, pp. 385-386.

5. *Ibid.*, p. 386.

6. *Ibid.*, p. 406.

7. *ibid.*, p. 387.

8. *Ibid.*, p. 396.

9. Cuming, *Sketches*, p. 247.

10. Buck, *Planting of Civilization*, p. 397.

11. Cuming, *Sketches*, p. 255.

12. Cf. James M. Miller, *The Genesis of Western Culture. The Upper Ohio Valley, 1800-1825. Ohio State Historical Collections*, IX (Columbus, 1938), 22-26, 77-80, 147-149.

13. *Ibid.*, pp. 39-40.

14. Joseph Schafer, "Beginnings of Civilization in the Old Northwest," *The Wisconsin Magazine of History*, XXI (1937-38), 212-236.

15. Cf. Lois K. Mathews, *The Expansion of New England: The Spread of New England Settlements and Institutions to the Mississippi River, 1620-1865* (Boston and New York, 1909), pp. 177, 267.

16. Beverley W. Bond, Jr., *The Civilization of the Old Northwest* (New York, 1934), p. 11.

17. Cuming, *Sketches*, p. 124.

18. Bond, *Civilization*, p. 20.

19. Miller, *Genesis*, p. 28.

20. W. H. Venable, *Beginnnings of Literary Culture in the Ohio Valley* (Cincinnati, 1891), p. 173.

21. Daniel Drake, *Natural and Statistical View or Picture of Cincinnati and the Miami Country* (Cincinnati, 1815), pp. 169-170.

22. Miller, *Genesis*, p. 33.

23. Drake, *View or Picture of Cincinnati*, p. 147.

24. *Ibid.*, p. 166.

25. *Ibid.*, p. 167.

26. W. W. Sweet, *The Story of Religions in America* (New York, 1930), p. 333: "The influence of the revivals upon western society was both good and evil, with good predominating. The immediate effect on western morals was undoubtedly good." On the schisms that followed the Second Awakening, see Anton T. Boisen, "Divided Protestantism in a Midwest County. A

Study in the Natural History of Organized Religion," *The Journal of Religion*, XX (1940), 359-381. For this reference I am indebted to President Herman B Wells of Indiana University.

27. *Ibid.*, pp. 307-308.

28. *Ibid.*, p. 339.

29. D. C. Shilling, "Pioneer Schools and School Masters," *Ohio Archaeological and Historical Publications*, XXV (1916), 36-51.

30. Venable, *Beginnings of Literary Culture*, p. 183.

31. Jane Scherzer, "The Higher Education of Women in the Ohio Valley Previous to 1840," *Ohio Archaeological and Historical Publications* XXV (1916), 1-22.

32. Drake, *View or Picture of Cincinnati*, p. 159.

33. James H. Rodabaugh, *Robert Hamilton Bishop. Ohio Historical Collections*, IV (Columbus, 1935), 65.

34. Quoted by R. Carlyle Buley, *The Old Northwest: Pioneer Period, 1815-1840* (Bloomington, 1951), II, 387.

35. *Ibid.*, II, 387.

36. *Ibid.*, II, 389-390.

37. *Ibid.*, II, 408. The best succinct account of the growth of colleges in the Northwest is that by Professor Buley, pp. 399 ff.

38. An excellent account of Oberlin is to be found in Robert S. Fletcher, *A History of Oberlin from Its Foundation through the Civil War*, 2 vols. (Oberlin, 1942). See also Buley, *The Old Northwest*, II, 404-406, and Mathews, *Expansion of New England*, pp. 185-187.

39. Edmund Flagg, *The Far West* (New York, 1838) in Reuben G. Thwaites, *Early Western Travels, 1748-1846* (Cleveland, 1906), XXVI, 204. Also quoted in Miller, *Genesis*, p. 92.

40. Buley, *The Old Northwest*, II, 489.

41. Frances Trollope, *Domestic Manners of the Americans* (New York, 1949), pp. 92, 93.

42. *Ibid.*, p. 311.

43. Bond, *Civilization of Old Northwest*, II, 443.

44. *Ibid.*, p. 444.

45. Quoted by Buley, *Old Northwest*, II, 523, from John B. Dillon in *Logansport Canal Telegraph*, June 25, 1836.

46. Rusk, *Literature of the Middle Western Frontier*, I, 168 ff. See also Bertha-Monica Stearns, "Early Western Magazines for Ladies," *The Mississippi Valley Historical Review*, XVIII (1931-32), 319-330, and Buley, *Old Northwest*, II, 523-ff.

47. Rusk, *Literature of the Middle Western Frontier*, II, 1 ff.

48. Quoted by Venable, *Literary Culture*, p. 137.

49. *Ibid.*, p. 140.

50. Bond, *Civilization of the Old Northwest*, p. 432.

51. Drake, *View or Picture of Cincinnati*, p. 160.

52. Bond, *Civilization of the Old Northwest*, p. 463.

53. Rusk, *Literature of the Middle Western Frontier*, I, 413.

54. Leon Howard, "Literature and the Frontier: The Case of Sally Hastings," *E L H: A Journal of English Literary History* VII (1940), 68-82.

CHAPTER IV

1. For an excellent account of the mountain men see Robert G. Cleland, *This Reckless Breed of Men* (New York, 1950).

2. Detailed accounts of this phenomenon will be found in Albert Weinberg, *Manifest Destiny: A Study of Nationalist Expansion in American History* (Baltimore, 1935). See also Henry Nash Smith, *Virgin Land: The American West as Symbol and Myth* (Cambridge, Mass., 1950).

3. Robert G. Cleland, *From Wilderness to Empire* (New York, 1944), p. 239.

4. *Ibid.*, pp. 255-256.

5. Josiah Royce, *California from the Conquest of 1846 to the Second Vigilance Committee in San Francisco: A Study of American Character.* Ed. Robert G. Cleland (New York, 1948), p. 282.

6. *Ibid.*, p. 293.

7. Louise Amelia Knapp (Smith) Clappe, *The Shirley Letters from the California Mines, 1851-1852.* Ed. Carl I. Wheat (New York, 1949), p. 164.

8. Royce, *California,* p. 287.

9. The Act was codified in 1872 and now constitutes Section 4468 of the California Political Code. I am indebted to Mr. William Clary for calling my attention to this statute.

10. Sarah Royce, *A Frontier Lady: Recollections of the Gold Rush and Early California* (New Haven, 1932), pp. 129-30.

11. *Ibid.,* p. 81.

12. *Apron Full of Gold: The Letters of Mary Jane Megquier from San Francisco, 1849-1856.* Ed. Robert G. Cleland (San Marino, Calif., 1949), p. 26.

13. *Shirley Letters,* p. 137.

14. Quoted from the hotel proprietor's memoirs by William W. Ferrier, *Pioneer Church Beginnings and Educational Movements in California* (Berkeley, 1927), p. 33.

15. *Ibid.,* p. 26.

16. Quoted, *ibid.,* p. 59.

17. *Ibid.,* p. 27.

18. Ferrier wrote his *Pioneer Church Beginnings* as a corrective to Edward A. Wicher, *The Presbyterian Church in California, 1849-1927* (New York, 1927), which claimed for the Presbyterians the first organized church.

19. Ferrier, *Pioneer Church Beginnings,* p. 48.

20. William W. Ferrier, *Ninety Years of Education in California, 1846-1936* (Berkeley, 1937), pp. 36-37.

21. Royce, *California,* p. 314.

22. Quoted by Ferrier, *Ninety Years,* p. 9.

23. Quoted, *ibid.,* p. 11.

24. *Ibid.,* p. 143.

25. *Ibid.,* p. 187.

26. *Ibid.,* p. 189.

27. *Ibid.,* p. 181. Quoted from the published statement of the aims of the college.

28. *Ibid.,* p. 311.

29. Quoted by Ferrier, *Pioneer Church Beginnings,* p. 85.

30. Quoted by Ferrier, *Ninety Years,* pp. 183-184.

31. William W. Ferrier, *Origin and Development of the University of California* (Berkeley, 1930), p. 263.

32. *Ibid.,* p. 244.

33. Ferrier, *Ninety Years,* pp. 125, 206-207.

34. *Ibid.,* p. 253.

35. Charles Burt Sumner, *The Story of Pomona College* (Boston, 1914), p. 10.

36. Franklin Walker, *San Francisco's Literary Frontier* (New York, 1939), p. 14.

37. *Ibid.,* p. 22.

38. *Ibid.,* pp. 116-145.

39. *Ibid.,* p. 347.

40. Quoted, *ibid.,* p. 349, from the *Argonaut,* February 9, 1878.

41. George R. MacMinn, *The Theatre of the Golden Era in California* (Caldwell, Idaho, 1941), p. 22. Professor MacMinn in this volume gives an excellent and detailed account of theatrical entertainment in this period.

42. *Ibid.,* pp. 28-39.

43. *Ibid.,* pp. 84-109.

44. *Ibid.,* p. 266.

45. *Ibid.,* p. 86.

46. Quoted *ibid.,* p. 85 from *California inter Pocula* in Bancroft's *Works* (San Francisco, 1882-91), XXXV, 268.

47. *The Shirley Letters,* p. 61.

48. Flora Haines Apponyi, *The Libraries of California* (San Francisco, 1878), pp. 6-7.

49. *Ibid.,* pp. 92-93.

50. *Ibid.,* pp. 108-109.

51. *Ibid.,* p. 148.

52. John S. Hittell, *The Resources of California* (7th ed., San Francisco, 1879), p. 28.

53. An appraisal of and apologia for Bancroft may be found in John Walton Caughey, *Hubert Howe Bancroft, Historian of the West* (Berkeley, 1946).

54. John S. Hittell, *A Brief History of Culture* (New York, 1875), pp. 5, 278, 289, 291.

55. Royce, *California,* p. 394.

56. Walker, *San Francisco's Literary Frontier,* p. 394.

CHAPTER V

1. Some of the alterations caused by new conditions are suggested in Walter P. Webb, *The Great Frontier* (Boston, 1952), pp. 46-63, 86, 91.

2. *Letters of Robert Carter 1720-1727.* Ed. by Louis B. Wright (San Marino, Calif., 1940), p. 25. Letter dated July 14, 1720.

3. Colin Brummitt Goodykoontz, *Home Missions on the American Frontier* (Caldwell, Idaho, 1939), p. 151.

4. *Ibid.*, pp. 119-127; William W. Sweet, *Religion in the Development of American Culture, 1765-1840* (New York, 1952), pp. 146-153.

5. Quoted by Goodykoontz, *Home Missions*, p. 158.

6. Louis B. Wright, "John Wesley: Scholar and Critic," *The South Atlantic Quarterly*, XXIX (1930), 262-281.

7. Sweet, *Religion*, p. 150.

8. Quoted by Goodykoontz, *Home Missions*, p. 161.

9. *Ibid.*, p. 108.

10. Quoted by Donald G. Tewksbury, *The Founding of American Colleges and Universities before the Civil War with Particular Reference to the Religious Influences Bearing upon the College Movement* (New York, 1932), pp. 4-5.

11. E. E. Calkins, *They Broke the Prairies* (New York, 1937), p. 84, as quoted by Sweet, *Religion*, p. 171. For further information on the zeal of the churches to found colleges see Walter B. Posey, *The Presbyterian Church in the Old Southwest, 1778-1838* (Richmond, Va., 1952) and *The Development of Methodism in the Old Southwest 1783-1824* (Tuscaloosa, Ala., 1933), *passim*.

12. Tewksbury, *Founding of American Colleges*, p. 13, n. 40.

13. *Ibid.*, pp. 16-17.

14. *Ibid.*, p. 14.

15. *Ibid.*, pp. 12-13; quoted from Walter Lyman's *Address before the S.P.C.T.E.W., 1855*, pp. 15-17.

16. See Louis B. Wright, *Middle-Class Culture in Elizabethan England* (Chapel Hill, N. C., 1935), *passim*, and *Reli-*

gion and Empire: The Alliance between Piety and Commerce in English Expansion, 1558-1625 (Chapel Hill, N. C., 1942), *passim.*

17. Cf. Edward Everett Dale, "Teaching on the Prairie Plains, 1890-1900," *Mississippi Valley Historical Review,* XXXIII (1946), 293-307.

18. Sweet, *Religion,* p. 155.

19. George P. Jackson, *White Spirituals in the Southern Uplands* (Chapel Hill, N. C., 1933), pp. 3-24.

20. *Ibid.,* pp. 24-54.

21. Henry S. Burrage, *Baptist Hymn Writers and Their Hymns* (Portland, Maine, 1888), p. 255.

22. Howard Swan, *Music in the Southwest, 1825-1950* (San Marino, Calif., 1952), p. 3.

23. *Ibid.,* pp. 27-29.

24. Burrage, *Baptist Hymn Writers,* p. 255.

25. William P. Strickland, *History of the American Bible Society* (New York, 1856), pp. 27-52.

26. Carl Sandburg, *Abraham Lincoln, the Prairie Years* (New York, 1926), p. 264.

27. Edwin W. Rice, *The Sunday-School Movement 1780-1917 and the American Sunday-School Union, 1817-1917* (Philadelphia, 1917), p. 75.

28. *Ibid.,* pp. 94-100.

29. Henry C. Jennings, *The Methodist Book Concern* (New York and Cincinnati, 1924), pp. 46, 142-143.

30. Sweet, *Religion,* p. 139. For a discussion of the churches as moral courts, see pp. 137-146.

CHAPTER VI

1. Howard Mumford Jones, *Ideas in America* (Cambridge, Mass., 1944) pp. 5-7.

2. John S. Hittell, *The Resources of California* (7th ed., San Francisco, 1879), p. 58.

3. *Ibid.,* p. 35.

4. *Winthrop Papers,* II, 1623-1630. The Massachusetts Historical Society (1931), p. 106.

5. See Louis B. Wright, "The Purposeful Reading of Our Colonial Ancestors," *E L H, A Journal of English Literary History*, IV (1937), 85-111.

6. Edition of 1630, p. 220.

7. David A. Lockmiller, *Sir William Blackstone* (Chapel Hill, N. C., 1938), p. 170.

8. Cf. Merle Curti, "The Great Mr. Locke, America's Philosopher, 1783-1861," *The Huntington Library Bulletin*, No. 11 (1937), 107-151.

9. Cf. Esther Cloudman Dunn, *Shakespeare in America* (New York, 1939), *passim*.

10. Ralph Leslie Rusk, *Literature of the Middle Western Frontier* (New York, 1926), II, 1-30.

11. Clifton Johnson, *Old-Time Schools and School-Books* (New York, 1935), p. 49.

12. From the title page of an edition of 1760 in the Library of Congress.

13. Johnson, *Old-Time Schools*, p. 71.

14. *Ibid.*, p. 96.

15. *Ibid.*, p. 321. Quoted from an 1800 edition of *Geography Made Easy*.

16. Richard D. Mosier, *Making the American Mind: Social and Moral Ideas in the McGuffey Readers* (New York, 1947), p. 34.

17. Ralph Leslie Rusk, *Literature of the Middle Western Frontier* (New York 1926), I, 269.

18. Hamlin Garland, *A Son of the Middle Border* (New York, 1923), p. 113.

19. Grace Gates Courtney, *History of Indiana Federation of Clubs* (Fort Wayne, Indiana, 1939), p. 8.

20. Mrs. J. C. Croly, *The History of the Woman's Club Movement in America* (New York, 1898), p. 680.

21. *Ibid.*, p. 325. Scattered through this chronicle of women's clubs, arranged by states, are numerous references to the interest in English history and English literature.

22. *Ibid.*, pp. 451-452.

23. *Ibid.*, p. 480.

24. W. H. Venable, *Beginnings of Literary Culture in the Ohio Valley* (Cincinnati, 1891), pp. 249-250.

25. Quoted, *ibid.*, pp. 250-251.

26. Quoted, *ibid.*, pp. 251-252.

27. For this and other information concerning the lyceum, I am indebted to Professor Carl Bode. The quotation from Holbrook is from *Niles Weekly Register*, XLVI (1834), 445-446.

28. Quoted by David Mead, *Yankee Eloquence in the Middle West: The Ohio Lyceum, 1850-1870* (East Lansing, Mich., 1951), p. 179.

29. *Ibid.*, p. 39.

30. *Ibid.*, p. 88.

31. *Ibid.*, pp. 145-146.

32. Hector St. John De Crèvecoeur, *Letters from an American Farmer* (1782) Everyman Series (London, 1945), p. 41.

33. Gerald W. Johnson, *Our English Heritage* (Philadelphia and New York, 1949), pp. 237-238.

34. *Ibid.*, p. 243.

Index

Index

HARPER TORCHBOOKS / The Bollingen Library

HARPER TORCHBOOKS / The Academy Library

HARPER TORCHBOOKS / The Science Library

HARPER TORCHBOOKS / The Cloister Library